Emotional Intelligence

And How To Achieve Mastery

25 Proven Ways To Improve Your People
Skills And Boost Your EQ For Work And
Life

Table of Contents

This space here is just so it can be a candid introduction to the author's other works

Please hop on over to Amazon to peruse them

Manipulation : Learn To Spot Manipulation As An Empath

Introduction

Ever been in one of those days where you just seemed to be getting on the wrong side of everyone? Heck, you might have even felt that you were getting on the wrong side of yourself! Being angry, seething with rage and frustration for the whole day. That does not sound very good does it?

Now picture this, what if you got out of bed feeling a little down and out of sorts. Maybe it's that big project dateline looming or that fearsome meeting with the Boss. Or it might just be the after effects of that hurricane like argument you had with your partner last night. Whatever it is, you know in the pit of your stomach that this mood really had the potential to ruin your day. It might end up like what happens earlier – stepping on everyone's toes and clipping your own wings. Or it might be a case where you actually know what is going on, and are able to masterfully handle your own emotions.

You have just defused a potential time bomb, and it all came down to your knowledge and understanding of your very own emotions.

How would you like to at least have a chance to know what to do, and how to do it whenever emotions threaten to boil over and actually start impacting your business and personal relationships? With this book, you are actually well placed to begin exploring how to do that.

You are probably quite a logical person. You may know what two and two equals, but how emotionally intelligent are you? Do you feel that you are in control of your emotions, or do they sneak up on you when you are not prepared? What about the emotions of other people? Are you capable of handling them and calming situations? If you can do either of these, then you are heading toward emotional intelligence, although many cannot do this balancing act. They are too self-absorbed and let their emotions rule their lives, or they are intolerant of others and lack empathy.

Imagine a manager in a business. He has to have a certain amount of emotional intelligence to be able to get the most from his workforce. That means being able to do the following:

- Able to use active listening

- Able to diffuse difficult situations

- Able to control his own emotions

Bosses who do not possess these abilities are not very good bosses and we all know them. These are people who are too egoist or who don't keep staff very long because their only view toward colleagues is that they are at work for a purpose and nothing else. They forget that people are also human beings with emotional responses. However, when you find entrepreneurs these days that do well for themselves, what you find as well is that colleagues and friends are happy to praise those bosses who inspire them. I remember seeing an article once where people who work with Richard Branson were telling readers about the positive energy they were able to get from his leadership. He himself said in the same interview that he employed people who were energetic and clever because it allowed him to place trust in others who could do specific jobs better than he could. Thus, one can see that emotional intelligence means being able to understand the needs of employees and balance them with the needs of the business. On a personal basis, people who exercise emotional intelligence will show the following traits:

- They will listen to others

- They will know how to empathize

- They are genuine people who can be trusted

There's something else that sets emotionally intelligent people apart from those who do not have this gift. Emotionally intelligent people are aware of their own strengths and weaknesses and can use different emotions to advantage. For example, a poet may be aware that he writes better when he is upset. A mathematician may realize that his powers of analytical investigation are better when he is depressed.

Emotional intelligence helps in so many ways because it makes the path through the maze of life easier and if you can foster this kind of emotional intelligence and make it part of your life, you will not only get on better with people, but you are also likely to put yourself in a direct line for promotion and be able to achieve more than those around you who don't have this gift.

It is not something that gains you qualifications, but it is something that gains you a quality of life. Those who have a high IQ are different from those who have a high level of EI or emotional intelligence and, in the coming chapters, you will be able to test your abilities and try to improve upon them, using your emotional intelligence to help you.

Emotional intelligence keeps you in control of your life in a good way. You will find all the triggers that start your emotions stirring are within your control when you have analyzed them and knew how to control them. The chapters that follow will help you to be able to not only control your emotions but enjoy them as well because you will be more positive in your life and your approach will be very different. In fact, you may enjoy seeing the positive person that you are becoming.

You will learn how to control your emotions and how to judge the emotions of others so that you can respond to them in an appropriate way, instead of letting your emotions take control of you and your potential actions toward others.

Value Time

Same as for my other book

Manipulation : How To Spot Manipulation as an Empath

I have also created an Audio book version for this same book on Emotional Intelligence

You can go over to Audible to check it out where it is

Available to Any Audible Subscriber For Free!

You can just subscribe if you haven't on a Free 30 day Trial and get this audiobook with the credit that they provide!

Chapter 1: What Is This EQ All About

How does emotional quotient differ from intelligence quotient? The simple answer is- they measure different forms of intelligence. Your technical acumen or technical skills is a direct result of a high intelligence quotient. You've mastered your skills well, which is a reflection of well-developed cognitive abilities. However, is intelligent quotient enough to determine your success when it comes to dealing with people (unless you are cooped up on a remote island all yourself, you have to deal with people)?

While intelligence quotient measures your technical expertise, emotional quotient evaluates your ability to manage your and other people's emotions in your work and personal life. You know where every employee stands when it comes to technical prowess but do you really understand their thoughts, actions and feelings to be able to better manage your and their behavior in sync with these emotions. When we gain insights into the underlying emotional patterns of people, it becomes easier to relate to them and channelize more productive behavior. This is a fundamental difference between intelligence quotient and emotional quotient.

Ever wondered why some of the cleverest people hit a blank in their professional lives and just can't seem to climb the corporate ladder, while the less knowledgeable and inexperienced folks smoothly sail their way to professional success? We all know of people who don't exactly possess the slickest technical skills yet surprisingly manage to reach top management positions. What is it that sets them apart from their more technically competent peers? Emotional intelligence is the key. It is their ability to recognize and control their and other's emotions to build more productive relationships that helps them score.

A person's intelligence quotient demonstrates their core technical competencies, cognitive development and unusual abilities, their emotional intelligence determines their ability to identify emotions and deal with others. Your emotional quotient determines how you will deal with stress, difficult people, bullying, high pressure work situations, conflict within the team, and differences in relationships.

Intelligence is an indicator of your cognitive prowess such as logical thinking, analytical reasoning, memorizing information, solving problems, verbal abilities, creative thinking and much more. Emotional intelligence is controlling your and other's emotions for creating optimally positive circumstances. Starkly different from your ability to comprehend words and numbers, emotional quotient helps you develop healthy interpersonal relationships in your personal and work life.

Emotional intelligence can include stress management, intuition, emotional flexibility, empathy, honestly and more. Emotional quotient highlights your and others emotions with respect to changing circumstances and people, while intelligence quotient is all about cognitive abilities.

While intelligence quotient can determine your success during your academic stint, emotional quotient is vital for all round success in life. You may excel as a student if you possess a high intelligence quotient. However to attain overall success in life, you need a high emotional quotient.

Research has indicated that there are five fundamental skills that distinguish the star performers from low performers. These skills are empathy, self-awareness, assertiveness, problem solving and happiness. Potential recruits who score high on these five attributes are 2.7 times likelier to succeed than folks who bag low scores.

So, why is emotional quotient so closely associated with a person's chances of becoming successful in life? The answer is – awareness of emotions and ability to express themselves confidently. Emotionally intelligent people are experts in gauging people's emotions and altering their pitches/presentations accordingly. Little wonder then that emotionally intelligence is so vital for people in sales, customer service, counseling and other industries.

For instance, a study closely followed the recruitment of sales personnel for cosmetic giant L'Oreal based on their emotional skills. It was observed that these emotionally competent sales people outdid other salespersons by a whopping $91,370 to amass a net revenue growth of $ 2,558, 360. In another research, a national insurance firm discovered that salespersons who were low on emotional skills like initiative, confidence and empathy sold far less policies (average premium of $54,000) that agents who scored high on emotional skills (average premium of $114,000). You get the picture, right? When you show high emotional competencies by being proactive, self confident and empathetic, you are able to connect to potential buyers and help them buy rather than simply sell.

In the workplace, intelligence quotient helps for analyzing, connecting the dots and undertaking research and development. Emotional intelligence is about forging a strong team spirit, leadership, building successful professional relationships, collaboration, service and initiative. Emotional quotient can be gained and enhanced as opposed to intelligence quotient, which is a more inborn and hereditary characteristic.

The goal for businesses isn't to simply hire people who are intellectually competent, but lack emotional or people skills. Today's competitive and social interactions dominated world demands workers who are smart (that's a given), and endowed with more thoughtfulness. The ideal candidate is a combination of emotional intelligence and general intelligence. Since all candidates applying for a position possess more or less the same technical competence, emotional intelligence often becomes a clinching factor when it comes to selecting people for important roles.

Standford-Binet, Woodcock-Johnson Tests of Cognitive abilities and Wechsler are some popular intelligence quotient tests, while Mayer-Salovey-Caruso Test and Daniel Goleman model score test are popular emotional intelligence assessment tests. An Intelligence Quotient test generally involves a collection of standardized questions where participants are assigned precise scores based on their answers. These scores are evaluated with respect to average scores within the age group to establish a person's intellectual capabilities.

Emotional quotient tests, on the other hand, are more challenging to administer because feelings and emotional skills are tougher to depict numerically. While intelligence quotient questions have a definite answer for every question, emotional quotient tests tend to be more subjective and require greater evaluation effort. Unlike IQ tests, there aren't any right or wrong answers. Respondents may not answer questions honestly simply to rank high or may adjust their responses according to what they are currently experiencing, which makes these results more skewed. There may be a tendency on part of the participant to say exactly what the evaluators want to hear rather than responding truthfully.

People possessing a high intelligence quotient are excellent at conducting tasks. They are quick absorbers of new skills and information. However, if they have a low emotional quotient, they tend to overlook their and other's feelings. For instance, when something doesn't turn out according to the way they wanted, these folks tend to lose their temper and lash out at people. While someone who is high on emotional intelligence will learn to control their emotions and get along with people around them. They are extremely effective when it comes to working as a team or working in a leadership role.

The concept of emotional intelligence has gained such a strong momentum that it has impacted a large a large number of areas including the corporate world. Several top organizations have now made emotional intelligence tests mandatory as part of the hiring process, along with intelligence quotient.

In personal relationships, 90 percent of the issues arise due to lack of emotional intelligence. Everything revolves around empathy, self awareness, awareness of the other person's emotions, understanding, communication patterns and the likes, which are all components of emotional intelligence.

Emotional quotient is not the antithesis of intelligence quotient. They aren't mutually exclusive. Some folks possess both in huge quantities, while others possess neither. Psychologists are keener to explore how the two attributes balance each other. For instance, how your ability to deal with stress impacts your ability to focus or learn new information.

The Three Models of Emotional Intelligence

The CEO of a tech company happened to stroll along the halls of his building, and he came across two developers with whom he wasn't impressed. He lashed out at them, and the two developers – a man and a woman – spent the rest of the day feeling terrible. When they each went home after work, their kids happily mobbed them. The woman was receptive to her kids' joy, but the man quickly dismissed his kids.

One thing stands out here: the woman was in a position wherein she can control her emotions; the man wasn't. He literally took out his frustrations with the CEO on his kids. Thus, we can infer that despite the man and woman having about the same intelligence quotient, considering that they work in a similar capacity, the woman has a higher emotional quotient.

Emotional intelligence is primarily the capacity of an individual to be aware of their emotions and the emotions of other people. An individual with a high emotional intelligence may discern between different feelings and control both how they express their feelings and how they react to other peoples' feelings.

The term "emotional intelligence" was first coined by a researcher named Michael Beldoch in 1964, but it became popular in 1995 when a science journalist named Daniel Goleman published a book titled Emotional Intelligence.

Today, emotional intelligence is categorized into three main models:

- Ability Model

- Mixed Model

- Trait Model

Ability Model

Peter Salovey of Yale University and John Mayer of the University of New Hampshire came up with the Ability

Model. They define emotional intelligence as "the capacity to think about emotions, and of emotions, to enhance thinking." This includes the capacity of an individual to recognize emotions, to access and produce emotions for thought purposes, to understand feelings and the emotional language, and to be in control of their emotions to advance both emotionally and mentally.

The Ability Model considers emotions to be an important source of information that helps an individual understand the world that they live in. According to the developers of this model, people have different capacities to process information that carries emotional undertones, and their ability to relate discernment of emotions to cognitive potential also varies. Here are the four main abilities that this model postulates:

• Perceiving emotions. This deals with a person's capability to spot and decode emotions in various things, people, and most importantly, yourself. The mere ability to recognize emotions is critical because it enhances the processing of any emotional information.

• Using emotions. This is about a person's capacity to tap into emotions to enhance cognitive functions like problem-solving, creativity, and critical thinking. Emotional intelligence enables a person to make the best of their situations based on the emotions generated.

• Understanding emotions. This relates to a person's capacity to understand the language of emotions. An individual with a high emotional intelligence is able to comprehend the emotional weight in every message. They are even proficient at detecting how emotions change in response to varying conditions.

•   Managing emotions. The last one is about our capacity to regulate our emotions and respond appropriately to the emotions of other people. An individual with a high emotional intelligence is in a position to control himself and to give an appropriate response in the face of other people's feelings.

This model has received both praise and criticism in the research community about its effectiveness.

Mixed Model

It is so named as the "Mixed Model" because it contains qualities of emotional intelligence and other personal traits that have no connection to emotions or intelligence. The Mixed Model is based on Daniel Goleman's idea of competencies and skills that drive performance. Some of these competencies include self-awareness, teamwork, motivation, service orientation, and initiative. Emotional competencies are not inborn. Rather, they are abilities that any person can develop with enough commitment and practice. Goleman proposed five categories where various emotional competencies fit.

•   Self-awareness. This is the ability to recognize your general emotional traits. A self-aware person has a strong sense of how to perceive and experience emotions. This is critical because it helps them make informed decisions. To be self-aware, you have to be confident first. An individual who is not ashamed of who they are gains a clear understanding of their emotions.

• Self-regulation. This is the ability to rein in oneself. When emotions are involved, logic is likely to disappear. Having this ability means being able to control yourself so as not to arrive at an undesirable outcome. Besides self-control, you also need to be honest and practice integrity, as well as to learn to adapt to various situations much quicker and utilize your creativity when you're in emotionally-volatile situations. Self-regulation also fosters the capacity of an individual to take responsibility for their actions.

• Motivation. This is the ability to pursue the various goals that you set for yourself. A motivated person harbors a lot more positive thinking and eliminates negativity. Even in the face of obstacles, a motivated person sticks to their goal and always takes the initiative. A motivated person is in perpetual search for tactics to improve their lives.

• Empathy. This is the capacity to discern other peoples' emotions and figure out the appropriate response. Empathy mainly stems from having political awareness and being willing and ready to be of service to other peoples' needs. An empathic person makes decisions that are aimed at connecting with other people and building them up.

• Social skills. This is the ability to relate to other people and establish relationships. Some of the competencies involved include collaboration, cooperation, influence, communication, conflict management, and building bonds.

Trait Model

This model postulates that emotional traits and emotional self-perceptions are ingrained in a person's personality. Therefore, emotional intelligence is how a person perceives their emotional abilities and behaviors. The key distinction is that this construct is not based upon any scientific basis but upon the individual's evaluation of oneself. This model is relatively new, having been published in 2009 by Petrides and his colleagues, and it is considered the answer to the ability-based construct. The Trait Model has received its fair share of praise and criticism as well.

Benefits of Emotional Intelligence

As discussed earlier, emotional intelligence is our ability to manage our and other's emotions by discriminating among these feelings, and using the information to guide our words, thoughts and actions. To cut a long story short, emotional intelligence is an aggregation of your mental and emotional skills. Emotionally intelligent people enjoy a multitude of benefits in all spheres of life including relationships, career and social life. Here are some ways in which your life can be impacted or benefited if you consciously focus on developing high emotional intelligence.

Greater Compassion in Personal and Work Life

One of the best benefits of high emotional intelligence is your ability to demonstrate more compassion for others both in the personal and professional sphere. This compassion allows them to connect with people at much deeper levels to forge meaningful relationships. Compassion can be manifested in several ways, including helping someone dealing with a personal issue by taking on their responsibilities or making small everyday decisions for the comfort/convenience of your employees.

Compassion helps you meaningfully connect with people both in your personal and professional life. You are able to reach out to people efficiently, forge more mutually fulfilling relationships and create an atmosphere of harmony and productivity. Emotional intelligence awards you greater compassion in dealing with people in various personal professional and social scenarios.

Fine Communication Skills

People with a well developed emotional quotient are more efficient when it comes to expressing themselves. They possess the ability to listen attentively to other people's verbal clues, while also tuning in to their non verbal communication. They know exactly what to say to channelize people's strengths. They use the right words and non verbal signals to help people feel at ease. There is little scope for misunderstanding whilst communicating with a person who has high emotional intelligence.

Emotionally intelligent people are well aware about the most compelling emotional triggers of the people around them. They know exactly how to inspire people to act. People who are able to communicate by emotionally connecting with are far more effective than technically competent folks who fail to demonstrate empathy while communicating with people. Emotional intelligence awards you better response skills.

Lower Chances of Addiction and Other Emotional Disorders

Addictions are generally a direct result of our inability to cope with emotions. People who struggle to come to terms with their emotions use addiction as a mechanism to avoid the more underlying and deeper prevailing issues. When you fail to recognize and manage negative emotions, there develops an unfortunate pattern of dependency on external factors such as food, nicotine, substance, alcohol, porn and the likes. Addiction is just a means to escape from emotions you aren't willing to deal with.

Emotionally intelligent folks are lesser prone to addiction because of their awareness of their emotions and the ability to manage these emotions. They have a solid understanding of their feelings, and do not struggle to deal with it. Since emotional intelligence makes you happier, more confident and balanced, there is a lesser propensity for dependence on destructive coping mechanisms. They adapt more easily to challenges and changing scenarios in life. Emotionally intelligent people are competent in resolving differences and coming up with more positive solutions. Since they display such a high understanding of their and other's emotions, it becomes easier for them to deal with conflicts.

Emotionally healthy people are less prone to be victims of drug abuse or binge eating disorders, which predominantly originate from much deeper psychological issues.

Coping With Life Challenges

Don't you sometimes look at some people and wonder how they are able to stay afloat through the most challenging situations and emerge even more successful than before? Chances are, these guys score high on emotional intelligence. Emotionally intelligent folks have the ability to calm their body and mind to view things from a clearer and more objective perspective. Their acts are more mindful and less panic struck.

Greater calmness, objectivity and clarity award you more resilience where life's challenges are concerned. Think about the kungfu fighter who can take on the most powerful opponents by constantly working on martial arts skills. Emotional intelligence equips you with those skills to take on the toughest challenges life throws at you with resilience.

Stellar Productivity

Emotional intelligence has a high correlation with an individual's work performance. Research has revealed that emotional intelligence is twice as crucial as technical/cognitive abilities even among professions such as engineering. Emotionally intelligent managers, supervisors and leaders are way more effective in managing teams, motivating people and negotiating.

They create a more positive atmosphere with happier workers, who are an asset to any organization. Happier workers translate into higher morale, low absenteeism, reduced attrition rate and higher productivity. This leads to happier customers, more sales and higher profits. Thus emotional intelligence is an invaluable trait when it comes to success at the workplace. Whilst everyone within an organization possesses more or less the same technical competency and educational qualifications, only a few rise up the corporate ladder because of their ability to manage people and their emotions.

An emotionally intelligent leader who understands the true value of identifying and managing emotions can empower his/her subordinates with these skills on a daily basis. Discipline or self regulation is essential when it comes to keeping your emotions in check, avoiding panic, remaining calm and being an asset to the team. Emotionally intelligent folks have little trouble in recognizing and managing potentially destructive emotions that can create stress and lower productivity. The approach is calmer, more confident and efficient. Rather than experiencing a more touchy view, these folks depend on their ability to possess a more realistic view of themselves and others.

Emotionally intelligent folks possess a highly evolved ability in recognizing and understanding factors that drive others, which makes them amazing leaders. They are able to make the most of this invaluable information to strengthen their loyalty and forge stronger relationships with people. A competent leader is intuitively tuned in to the most compelling aspirations and desires of his followers. He knows the "hot buttons" of his employees and exactly how to channelize these "hot buttons" to increase overall productivity and positivity within the work environment.

Emotionally intelligent leaders know how to channelize this information for extracting better performance/productivity from people and keeping them happy. People with a high emotional quotient excel at recognizing the strengths and weaknesses of people and harnessing an individual's virtues for benefiting the team.

High emotional intelligence creates better leaders who are able to inspire greater faith and loyalty by using their team's or follower's or emotional range. They are more aware of their emotions, which allow emotionally intelligent folks to create a harmonious environment. Practicing emotional intelligence makes you a better leader.

Did you know that 67% of all competencies said to be fundamental for high performance in the professional sphere is emotional intelligence? Take the example of the world's most successful CEOs. Amazon's Jeff Bezos passionately talks about getting right into the hearts of his customers in a 2009 YouTube video while announcing the company's Zappos acquisition. When Howard Schultz of Starbucks was a child, his father lost a health insurance claim. This turned him into one of the most empathetic CEOs, who is well known showing his employees thoughtfulness by offering generous healthcare rewards. Little wonder then that these folks are as successful as they are. They understand the emotional pulse of their employees and customers to keep them emotionally gratified.

Emotional intelligence helps in building emotional maturity, boosting social intelligence, preventing relationship problems, enhancing interpersonal communication, helping control emotions, dealing with stress, influencing leadership, helping authorities make sound business change decisions, supporting staff and controlling resistance to change.

Boosted Employee Morale and Lower Attrition

Morale may be an intangible concept in the corporate world but its effects are highly measureable. You may not realize the value of a high morale when it's there, but you will definitely know when it's missing. Think about the lateness, early departures, attrition, sick leaves your company suffers from. When leaders take the time to build emotional intelligence and connect with their team members, it reflects in the employee morale.

Emotionally intelligent leaders who build stronger emotional ties with subordinates witness improvement in the team's morale, lower measureable absenteeism, a higher team spirit and a greater desire to contribute to an organization's success. The emotional intelligence skill building cost can be minimal. However, the return on investment can be extremely high.

Let's get real here and call a spade a spade. Employees do not really quit roles, they quit senior managers. It is about escaping people and not positions. Emotionally intelligent leaders, who recognize emotional triggers, quickly pick up emotional clues of their team members and "customize" their approach to each member's unique emotional make-up and motivation will experience greater success in retaining employees. This should not be mistaken with not doing justice to one's own voice or feelings. It simply means, presenting an accurate emotional response towards each team member to treat them with greater compassion, respect and empathy.

The problem with most managers who do not understand the concept of emotional intelligence is that they use a one size fits all approach for dealing with all employees, without understanding the emotional framework, motivators and goals of individual team members. This one size fits all approach does not produce flattering results because personalities vary. Some people are more intrinsically motivated, while others thrive on extrinsic motivation. Some folks are quick to reveal their emotions; others aren't very comfortable sharing their feelings. Once you understand the emotional make-up of people, it becomes easy to deal with them more efficiently.

Chapter 2: EQ And Why You Want It

Social intelligence is characterized by the ability to build successful social relationships and overcome challenging social environments. It is our ability to connect with and deal with other people in a social set-up scenario. As a society, we are obsessed with intelligence and academic smartness. However, our relationships play a much bigger role in our overall development and well-being. Of course, you need to be academically sound to enjoy professional success but you also need to be socially smart to lead people and build strong relationships.

However, have you wondered what happens when you are not socially adept or intelligent?

Lack of Understanding of Other People's Emotions

A person I knew (let's call her Anne for this example) was exceptionally good where technical knowledge, ability and potential were concerned. Anne was able to get things done and drive commendable results. However, her approach to getting those results wasn't very favorable and didn't find many takers, which made her an unpopular manager. Anne was known to demean others, display impatience and sport a rather dogmatic attitude. She left a lot of people disappointed and unmotivated, which didn't go down well in her feedback. When confronted about the feedback others gave against her, Anne was shocked. She didn't see it this way and was surprised others found her dictatorial.

For Anne, she was only getting people to perform according to the demands of the projects. This lack of self-awareness and lack of understanding about how she impacted other people's emotions led to Anne's downfall. Imagine an otherwise ace professional struggling with lack of self-awareness and a sense of empathy.

What Anne was saying was, "At the end of it all, it is about results and getting stuff done." What her team and subordinates were interpreting was, "I don't care about anything but results, and in the process, if I hurt your feelings, it doesn't matter." There was a clear gap between what Anne thought she was coming across as and what she was actually coming across as. This disconnect is what caused her professional downfall!

Socially and emotionally intelligent people can identify not just their own feelings but also the impact they have on other people's emotions. They can recognize and perceive other people's emotions and manage them in the best interests of everyone involved. Unlike Anne, they know the impact their actions or emotions have on others and therefore, alter their own emotional behavior to positively influence other people's actions.

You may have all the intelligence, academic excellence and experience in the world, but if you don't know how to deal with your emotions and other people's emotions, you aren't going to get far in your professional and personal life.

Signs that you lack social and emotional intelligence:

•   You often think people are being too sensitive to your humor or jokes and are overreacting.

•   You jump into any conversation with absolute assertiveness and refuse to budge most of the time. You are also quick to defend your stand with gusto should anyone even question it reasonably.

•   You think social popularity and being liked in your workplace is grossly overrated. As long as you do your work and deliver results, it shouldn't matter whether people like you or not.

•   You have extremely high expectations of yourself and others, many times bordering on unreasonable and impractical.

•   You get irritated and frustrated when others expect you to understand how they feel. Your thought process is, "How am I supposed to know or understand someone else's feelings without them talking to me about it?"

•   Most of the time you feel like people don't understand your point or know where you are coming from, which makes you annoyed and upset.

- You always find yourself blaming other people and circumstances for your shortcomings and failures. You seldom accept responsibility and accountability for your acts, and you pass the buck elsewhere.

Of course, it isn't just limited to these signs. There are many other indicators of low social and emotional intelligence, though these are typical signs that most people with low emotional and social intelligence display.

Not Being Flexible or Agreeable

Be honest and answer this. Do you like people who always take the high road around you? Nope, no one does really! These are people who are extremely rigid about their views, are not open to suggestions, don't believe in working out a way to meet in the middle, and don't appreciate even constructive criticism from others. It is either my way or the highway for them. If you are one of these people, you are sooner or later going to struggle with social relationships. A huge component of emotional and social intelligence is being open, agreeable and flexible.

If you are a rigid and closed person, people may pretend to be nice to you on the outside but deep on the inside, they don't really appreciate your tendency to dictate terms all the time. Before you know it, they'll start avoiding you and minimizing interaction with you. Social intelligence is about accepting and respecting other people's perspectives even if it is different from your own. It is about being flexible enough to identify and incorporate the good in other people's suggestions. It helps you gain a different perspective and puts you on the same page as the other person to connect in a more harmonious manner. People will appreciate having you around them and listening to your perspective in an open and agreeable manner.

Social Anxiety and Social Triggers

People who lack social intelligence often become increasingly anxious in a social situation, which hinders their ability to connect with people.

What are the triggers that are causing this social anxiety? As a child, you may not have had many people attending your birthday party. This has been firmly embedded in your mind even though you've grown up now, and things have changed a lot. Today, you may have plenty of people who would willingly attend your party but disappointing and negative thoughts about your childhood birthday party prevent you from inviting your friends to celebrate with you.

Identifying your social triggers can help combat social anxiety.

•   What are the types of social situations that make you anxious?

•   What type of interactions make you want to quickly escape from the place?

•   When do you get a feeling that you can't really be yourself?

Socially anxious people find it challenging to conduct themselves in social scenarios, to fulfill social relationships and professionally network with people from within their industry. They are basically operating in isolation which doesn't help them leverage the power of social contacts and belonging in a community.

Lack of Empathy

Imagine a scenario where a person who is not socially intelligent comes to you and tries to offer condolences on the death of a family member. You get his or her phone call to offer condolence. They talk about how sorry they are for your loss but you get a feeling they don't really mean it and are doing it more out of a sense of obligation. You can hear them speaking to someone else in the background and typing on a keyboard—basically, they are preoccupied with something else and are only offering their regret about your loss as an obligation without actually empathizing with you. How do you end up feeling after the rather insincere, ice cold and mechanical condolence? It makes you feel even worse than you felt before they called.

Socially unintelligent folks lack the ability to empathize with other people and their troubles, which makes it challenging for them to form strong and mutually fulfilling bonds with others.

How Emotional Intelligence Affects Your Personal Life and Career

For the longest time, people hadn't been aware of the importance of emotional intelligence. The emphasis had been on IQ. People believed that IQ was the biggest – if not the only – requirement for achieving success.

Thanks to researchers like Daniel Goleman, the evidence has been dug out that emotional quotient is every bit as critical as intelligence quotient. People who have a high emotional intelligence enjoy a much rewarding life than their low-EQ counterparts. This is tied to their ability to understand and manage their feelings as well as the feelings of other people.

Personal Relationships

The most important relationship in society is the family unit. It takes a special kind of partnership to live together harmoniously and bring up a family.

Emotional intelligence is one of the vital ingredients of a stable family. For one, it allows you to lead by example. Children are highly impressionable; they never do as you tell them – they do as they see you do. A parent who leads by example acknowledges that they shoulder a huge responsibility towards their children. In this way, the children would have a good role model to imitate. You might also attempt to practice your values such that your partner would follow. For instance, if truth-telling is one of your values, you should see to it that you always tell the truth. In this way, you will challenge your spouse into always telling the truth as well.

Emotional intelligence promotes forgiveness. When two or more people form a relationship, one thing is to be expected: conflict. If the parties to that relationship have low emotional intelligence, they are likely to fight between themselves and may end up throwing away what they have. But if they have high emotional intelligence, they will surely give compassion a chance. Only emotionally strong people can afford to forgive.

Emotional intelligence strengthens relationships through honest communication, and communication is not just about opening your mouth and saying something. It encompasses verbal and nonverbal aspects, and most importantly, it must be honest. Both partners should be free to state their needs, wants, and problems.

Career

One of the areas where emotional intelligence makes a big impact is in your career. If you're like most people, your job must be demanding. The average employee calls it "stressful." But sadly, your success rate will be measured according to your ability to adapt to these unfavorable working conditions. And so, it takes emotional intelligence to survive in an environment that keeps you on your toes. Without emotional intelligence, you would likely become an underperforming employee, which makes you dispensable.

If you can achieve results in a high-stress environment, it is indicative of a high emotional intelligence. It doesn't mean that you cannot feel the stress, but it means that you acknowledge the stress and are not ready to let it bog you down. On the other hand, a person with low emotional intelligence tends to let every minor issue derail them. And the output of such an employee is going to be greatly affected. Keeping in mind the benefits of emotional intelligence, it is easy to see why a person with high emotional intelligence would receive a job promotion over a person who lacks it.

When you're working alongside other people, there will be instances when they will need you to be the bigger person. It's called the practice of empathy. As an empathetic individual, you have to show concern for your colleagues. Sometimes, they may be unable to deliver on a set task for whatever reason, but it is upon you to respond appropriately instead of criticizing them. When you show your colleagues empathy, you come across as being charismatic. And in such environments, having social capital is critical in advancing through the ranks. A person with low emotional intelligence would hardly notice a colleague in need, let alone offer empathy. They are unable to understand the feelings of another person.

Emotional intelligence also promotes problem-solving skills. In a work environment, you can expect controversies, arguments, and fights. Obviously, such conflicts should be resolved as quickly as possible because they hold back the workers from adding value to their time. It takes emotional intelligence to stop conflict and prevent similar outcomes in the future.

Creativity goes together with emotional intelligence. Creativity has a role to play in an amicable conflict resolution. Creating options when you resolve a conflict lessens the damage, if not eliminating it altogether. The only downside is that the success of your method greatly depends on the behaviors of the other parties. But even if you're up against non-cooperative colleagues, you can still be in control of your emotions and respond appropriately.

Emotional intelligence helps you make great career decisions. Well, you're always going to have to make decisions that impact your career. What is your basis for gauging the perfect job for you? Is it the salary, working environment, the boss, or the nature of the work? When it comes to career advancement, the stakes are high, and one wrong move could potentially ruin your career. So, you have to depend on your emotional intelligence to make the right choice.

The important career decisions are not only those that involve migrating jobs but also the decisions that touch upon skill improvement and team building. If you're low on emotional intelligence, you will hardly identify opportunities to advance your career. And in the instance where you have alternatives, you're likely to take the option that will flop. This is because of your one-sided inclination as opposed to taking all factors into consideration. For instance, if an employer A and an employer B offered you $100,000 and $150,000 salary respectively, you might be tempted to rush to employer B, failing to question other important factors.

Chapter 3: Those Things You Can Do For Your EQ

After gaining a thorough understanding of emotional intelligence and its benefits, the million dollar question is – is it really possible to improve one's emotional intelligence or emotional quotient? Is it possible from struggling to cope with your and other's emotions to being a rockstar at understanding emotions?

With all its advantages, who wouldn't want high emotional intelligence? Who wouldn't want greater professional success, business potential, leadership skills, relationship gratification, humor, good healthy, positivity and happiness around them? Think about an antidote that beats stress, helps you form rewarding relationships with people and much more.

Take any coaching intervention program, and it will generally highlight some aspect of emotional intelligence in the name of interpersonal skills or social/soft skills. The most compelling reason for this is that, while intelligence quotient is tough to change, emotional quotient can be acquired with training and consistent practice. So, the good news is that even if you do not consider yourself very emotionally evolved, there is plenty of scope to boost your emotional quotient with practice, training and conscious effort.

The best part about enhancing your emotional intelligence is that it can be practiced in your everyday life. For instance, if you are short tempered, start by showing greater empathy or being a more considerate listener.

Respond Rather Than React

Reacting is a more unconscious and uncontrolled process that is a result of an emotional trigger. For instance, you snap when someone annoys you or you are already stressed due to another reason.

Responding, on the other hand, is more controlled and something you choose to do. You decide exactly how you behave in the given situation. For example, explaining to someone that you are not feeling too good and that this isn't the best time to interrupt you, and that later you'd be in a much better position to give them a good hearing. You've simply chosen to deal with the situation in a more productive and less impulsive manner by taking control of your emotions.

Evaluate how your actions will impact others before acting. If your behavior will affect others, try and place yourself in their shoes. How are they bound to feel if you say or do something? Would you like to go through the experience yourself? If you have to take a particular action, can you help people in coping with its effects?

Emotional Quotient Is Not Rigid

Though our capacity to recognize and handle our and other's emotions is largely determined by childhood experiences, heredity and other factors, it isn't rigid. We can alter our ability to comprehend and manage emotions over the long term with the right coaching and dedication. You can change of course, however, the question is do you want to change? Are you willing to put in the effort required to be more emotionally intelligent? Sometimes, while you may successfully be able to manage your external emotions, you may still grapple with emotions you do not manage to display on the outside.

While some folks are naturally positive, calm and social, others can be plain grumpy, egoistic, shy or insecure. However, no trait is unchangeable. If you truly want to change an aspect of your personality, you can. Emotional intelligence naturally increases with age, without any intervention. This is the rationale behind the popular belief that people gain more maturity as they grow older. Overall, yes it is possible to improve your emotional quotient over the long term with intervention, guidance and regular practice.

Some Methods Work More Efficiently Than Others

Some techniques for boosting emotional intelligence such as cognitive behavioral therapy for better psychological flexibility can work better than other methods. Since emotional intelligence is linked to human behavior, it can never be an exact science. The dynamics of human behavior, motivation, communication and feelings will keep changing. You have to identify and evaluate what works for you. While behavioral therapy works wonderfully well for some people, others may find meditation or deep breathing more effective in calming their emotions.

Here are some tried and tested tips for being the ultimate emotional intelligence ninja.

Accurate Feedback

One of the most crucial aspects if you want to enhance your emotional quotient through any coaching intervention or self practice program is accurate feedback. People generally do not realize how others perceive them, especially people in senior management positions in organizations.

Though these folks are increasingly motivated, responsible and high on technical skills, they rarely take the time to pause and assess their behavior. In a nutshell, we do not possess a very accurate notion of how nice we come across as. Wishful thinking, misplaced optimism and overconfidence can be factors contributing to this blind spot.

Generally people tend to over evaluate themselves in the niceness department. They believe they are nicer than they actually are. Any effort at increasing your emotional quotient must begin with gaining a thorough understanding your strengths and weaknesses. Use valid and genuine assessment techniques like personality tests or accurate feedback to determine your success with developing a higher emotional quotient.

Pay Close Attention to Your Behavior

You can only manage your emotions more effectively if you are consciously aware of it. It starts with paying very close attention to your emotions and their impact on your behavior. Emotional awareness is one of the cornerstones of EQ.

Start noticing how you act when you experience specific situations, and how it affects your everyday life. Do these feelings impact your productivity? How about your communication with other people? Do your emotions pose a threat to your overall well-being, including your physical and emotional health? How do you react when you are extremely angry, happy or sad? Once you are consciously aware of your reactions to emotions, you will be able to wield better control over them and channelize them more productively.

Use Your Mental Pause Button

Use your mental pause button each time you find yourself on the verge of speaking or acting. Take a moment, breathe deeply and think before you respond. Whenever you feel tempted to type an elaborate mail in rage, stop and think if it is going to help resolve the issue or only make it worse. Each time you feel like screaming at someone or making a combustible comment on the social media, apply the pause button.

When you consciously work on pausing before you speak or act, you get into the habit of thinking before acting or speaking in a manner that can worsen any situation. You learn to manage, control and tackle your emotions to handle any situation in a more constructive manner. When you learn to use this technique, you realize that the button to your feelings and emotions is in your hands.

When you sense a challenge in controlling impulses, deal with it by quickly diverting your attention. Distract your thoughts by counting or concentrating on a pre-planned diversion thought. Your mind can be trained to shift thoughts or conversations fast.

Emotional Intelligence Be Developed

Our emotional intelligence pathway originates within the brain going right down to the spinal cord. The primary senses are involved here and must go to the brain's front portion before you start thinking logically or rationally about an occurrence. Emotions are generated in our limbic system, which is why our emotional response to an incident occurs before the rational mind gets involved. Emotional intelligence is based on efficient communication patterns between the brain's logical and emotional points.

Have you heard of plasticity? It is a term used by neurologists for describing the brain's ability to keep evolving and changing. The brain keeps growing newer connections as we acquire new skills. The change is slow, as the brain keeps developing more and more connections to boost its efficiency.

When you use various strategies for boosting emotional intelligence, you are actually letting the microscopic neurons (billions of them) lined between the emotional and logical centers of the brain to branch into smaller arms that touch other cells. This simply means, one cell can form more than 15,000 connections. The chain reaction signifies that it is simpler for the brain to adapt to this new behavior in the long term. Once the brain is trained with the help of emotional intelligence strategies, it becomes a habitual behavior/thought pattern.

Be Open to Feedback

Boost your emotional intelligence by being more receptive to feedback. While you may disagree with the criticism/feedback, sometimes being open to other's views can help you identify behavior patterns that may be having an effect that you didn't intend. Healthy feedback can guard you from blind spots and adjust your behavior.

The more you exist in denial mode about destructive behavior, the more challenging it may be for you to develop a high emotional quotient. Acceptance and awareness is the key to increasing your emotional intelligence.

Read Body Language

Try to gauge people's innermost emotions by tuning in to their body language. Pick up clues about their emotional health by observing their body language. Sometimes people say something while their expressions and gestures convey the opposite or a deeper truth they aren't comfortable revealing. When you practice being more mindful of their body language, you tap into their true emotional fabric to adapt you responses and reactions. Sometimes people resort to less conspicuous ways for communicating their emotions.

For instance, a person may try saying something reassuring but the high tone of their voice may defeat those words and indicate high stress. These are small yet powerful indicators of people's behavior patterns and reading them correctly will give you the power to unlock other's emotional framework.

Be Positive and Happy

How would you rate your happiness quotient on a scale of 1 to 10? Emotional intelligence originates from being happy and vice versa. They aren't simply happy because good things are happening to them but because they are great at managing and taking control of their own happiness.

Happiness originates from within. A person who is capable of managing his emotions efficiently wakes up joyfully each morning. These people encounter challenges too, just like everyone else. However, they do not let these issues dampen their zest for positivity. Develop greater emotional intelligence by keeping your mind clear, avoid getting caught in destructive self-pity and take charge of your happiness. Emotional intelligence comes with being more positive and solution oriented.

Happy people gain more appreciation and following from people to help them tide over tough times. They spread more happiness, live longer and come up with constructive solution. It is a misconception that happiness is a result of material possessions. Genuinely happy people are those who can manage their emotions well, spread happiness, and most importantly those who focus on giving rather than receiving. Emotionally intelligent people know that it costs zilch to be happy and yet the returns are invaluable.

Avoid Labeling Your Emotions

All your emotions are valid, including the not so positive ones. Avoid assigning labels and judging your emotions. When you judge your feelings, you inhibit your ability to experience them. When you cannot fully express or experience something, you prevent yourself from using these emotions more positively.

Each emotion you experience is a vital piece of information closely linked with what is happening around you and how it affects you. Without information about your emotions, you'd be left clueless about how to react to your emotions and manage them more effectively.

Connect negative feelings to events but avoid judging them to gain a better understanding. For instance, if you feel envious, try and figure out what the emotions is conveying to you about the situation. Learn to experience positive emotions so you recognize each opportunity to feel them to the fullest.

Practice Empathy

Empathy is all about trying to understand why someone feels or acts in the way they do by putting yourself in their shoes. It is also being able to communicate this understanding to them more effectively. Empathy can also apply to your emotions and feelings.

Each time you notice yourself experiencing a specific emotion or behavior, try and think why you feel the way you do. You may not be able to figure it out at the onset but pay close attention and you'll start receiving various answers that you didn't notice earlier.

When someone is experiencing a rather strong feeling, ask yourself how you would feel in a similar scenario. Always be interested in what people say to respond in a more sensitive manner. It is always a good practice to ask questions and summarize what people say so you are clear, and people know you are actively listening to them.

When you put yourself in the other person's shoe, you reduce reactivity. For instance, if your child is resisting something you are telling him/her, try thinking it isn't easy for them to deal with peer pressure and academics. Think for a moment how it must be to be a young kid in the current competitive age.

If your manager is being demanding and difficult, think about the pressure of performance expectation they are dealing with at the hands of senior management. When you start thinking more objectively by considering where the other person is coming from, understanding and conflict resolution become much simpler.

Managing other's emotions requires maturity, skill and tact. It starts by being aware of exactly where you want the person to go? Do you want to lead them to feeling happier, calmer, more aware, secure, vigilant or cautious, for instance? Once you realize how they are feeling and how to lead them there, you will know what to say and do.

We tend to forget how particular experiences feel; even we've lived through it ourselves. You can only imagine how much perspective limiting it becomes if we've not experienced what the other person is going through. What is the best way to bridge this gap? The nucleus of empathy lies in understanding the "why" among other things. Why does this person feel the way they do? What are they dealing with that I fail to see? Why do I experience different feelings than them? Explore your "whys" and you will be well on your way to better understanding the feelings of others.

Being kind, considerate and helpful is one of the best ways of practicing emotional intelligence.

Be Assertive

Emotionally intelligent folks know the importance of setting appropriate boundaries to let people know our stand. You have the right to disagree with people without acting in a disagreeable manner. Learn to say refuse without feeling guilty when you are not up to something or you find people taking advantage of you. Set your priorities and safeguard yourself from stress, harm and duress.

Rather than using "you" followed by the accusation and putting people on the defensive foot, try making them more open to listening to and understanding your point. For instance, instead of saying "you should do this" or "you are xyx", try saying, "I feel really uncomfortable when you expect me to do this over my priorities" or "I strongly believe that I deserve recognition from the organization based on my consistent performance and contributions." See what we did there? We aren't putting people on the defensive by pointing a finger at them and saying, "you did this" or "you are like this." We are being assertive and talking about our feelings without blaming anybody.

Accept Responsibility for Your Feelings and Actions

This can be one of the most challenging yet productive tips for boost your emotional quotient. Your emotions originate from you and therefore you are completely responsible for them.

People around you may be responsible for creating certain situations but it is ultimately you who are in charge of your reaction to those situations. You may not always be able to control how others around you speak or behave. However, the way you react to their words and actions is something you have control over.

If you are hurt by someone and lash out, you are the one responsible for it. Get out of the mindset that "someone makes you do something." No one can make you angry; you are responsible for your anger. No one holds the strings to your emotions. No one makes you do or feel anything. Your reaction is completely your own responsibility. Your feelings can offer you important guidelines about your experience with different people along with your own requirements and preferences. However, your feelings and actions are no one's but your responsibility.

Once you start accepting responsibility for your feelings and behavior, it becomes simpler to manage it for impacting all spheres of your life positively.

If you hurt people, be gracious enough to accept it and apologize. Ignoring the person or not accepting the responsibility for your behavior is not a sign of high emotional intelligence. Your relationships will be much more positive and people will forgive you more easily if you make an honest attempt to set things right rather than live in denial land. Accepting your mistakes, apologizing and moving on is a sign of high emotional intelligence.

Practice Being More Light Hearted

When you are more light hearted and optimistic, it is simpler to capture the goodness of everyday situations and objects. Positivity results in greater emotional happiness and increased opportunities. People are forever looking to be around optimistic folks who come up with positive connections and possibilities. When you become more negative, you only concentrate on what can go awry rather than building strong resistance.

People with a more evolved emotional quotient know how to utilize wit and humor to make everyone feel happier, positive and safer. They know the art of using laugher to tide over tough times.

Practice Deep Breathing

Strong emotions impact us physically too. When we are stressed or anxious, our bodies respond in a more evolutionary instinctive manner like we're face to face with a nature based threat. The physical reactions include constricted blood vessels, shallow breathing and speedier heart rate.

When we learn to consciously manage our body's reaction to anxiety, the emotional attribute is lowered. Each time you feel nervous or tense, practice slow and deep breathing. Concentrate on the flow of the breath and the abdominal cavity. You will invariably feel better and calmer once you relax and create more space in your mind.

Mindfulness or mindful breathing is another way to achieve stillness of the mind by completely immersing yourself in the present non-judgmentally. When you get into the habit of identifying your thoughts and emotions with judgment, you boost your awareness and gain greater clarity rather than operating from a judgmental and assumption laden point of view. Mindfulness reduces your chances of being overtaken by negative or destructive emotions.

Decrease Negative Personalization

When we feel negatively impacted by someone's behavior, do not rush into a conclusion. Tempting as it is to ascribe a negative reason for their behavior, try to gather a more holistic perspective of the circumstances before reacting. For instance, it is easy to think a friend isn't returning your call or message because he/she wants to avoid you.

However, they may also be busy or ill or in a dire situation. When we avoid ascribing negative reasons or personalizing people's behavior, we view them more objectively and with less hateful/judgmental emotions. The ability to overcome negative personalization of people's behavior is critical for boosting your emotional quotient.

Develop Flexibility

Sometimes we get stuck in our own monotonous traps and become rigid and inflexible, which may impair our emotional intelligence. People with a highly developed emotional quotient know when to adapt and keep pace with newer techniques rather than getting stuck in an increasingly unproductive cycle. They know when how to adapt and manage their emotions according to the situation. Emotionally intelligent folks know when to adapt and shift perceptions.

Those who possess a highly developed emotional quotient are always open to newer experiences, challenging opportunities and a variety of adventures. Be open to change and shed the uneasiness and inhibitions attached with change.

Learn to decipher the consequences of your words and behavior. Emotionally intelligent folks pick their battles very selectively. They realize that peace and relationships are more valuable than being right.

When you learn to evaluate the consequences of your words and actions and demonstrate more flexibility and adaptability in your actions/words, you display high emotional intelligence. This isn't to be mistaken with letting people walk all over you. By all means, be assertive. However, know that it's not about being right or winning arguments all the time. Emotional intelligence is being perspective enough to realize what is worth fighting for and what is worth giving up.

Practice Active Listening

During arguments or disagreements we often listen not to understand but to react and respond. When the other person is speaking, we are almost mentally constructing out own arguments to answer back or give back to them. This leads to even more conflict.

Dealing with conflict becomes more effective when you tackle issues in an assertive yet respective manner, without being defensive. When you listen empathetically, your own thoughts and emotions are taken into account. Listening actively and empathetically can help you shed toxic feelings building up in you.

Be assertive by all means, but also practice active listening to find that one point that can lead to resolution. Problem solution only happens when you understand where the other person is coming from and what they want. You can find a middle ground only when you tune in to the words, feelings and emotions of the other person, not just to give a fitting reply but also to resolve the issue. Listening is all about putting the other person's words, thoughts and feelings first.

Your opinion about people or events may not change. However, the time spent listening to the other person may just calm you and help you come up with a more positive or constructive response. It may help you see things from a different perspective and analyze the situation more objectively.

Resolve Conflicts Like a Boss

One of the best tips for developing high emotional quotient is mastering conflict management skills. Conflict resolution actually puts your emotional intelligence to practical use. Resolving differences and conflicts involves many aspects including identifying feelings, clear expression of thoughts, active listening, staying calm and coming up with a solution that diffuses the situation rather than escalating it. When we struggle to understand and control our feeling, we experience a sense of irritation, depression and erratic behavior patterns. Conflicts only get magnified, making it all the more stressful for to deal with. Once you recognize yours and other's emotions, and learn to manage them, you enjoy a happier and more balanced life.

Be Emotionally Honest

Be emotionally honest and transparent. You are not communicating genuinely if you shut yourself off from expressing emotions. If you say you are alright with a sorrowful face, you are being dishonest in your communication. When you practice being more real about emotions, it is easier for people to read it. It is always great to be able to be yourself and share your real feelings. It helps people know your feelings and understand where you are coming from. They trust you more, which sets the base for more rewarding relationships.

By all means manage your emotions so as to avoid hurting others but misleading others about your emotions or denying real deeper emotions is not a sign of high emotional intelligence.

Stop Complaining

One of the first steps towards boosting your emotional intelligence is to stop complaining. Shed the victim syndrome and know that the solution to your problem is well within your grasp. Emotionally intelligent people rarely blame others or their circumstances for the challenges in their life. Instead, they search for matured ways to dissolve a relationship or talk to people who've wronged them in private. They also have a steady stream of effective coping mechanisms such as yoga, meditation, nature trips or simply venting their feelings by writing.

Listen to Physical Clues

Some of the best indicators of our emotional condition are the physical signals our body gives us. You can develop a greater awareness of your emotions simply by tuning in to your physical sensations. You may feel a knot in your tummy while commuting to work, which can be a sign of high stress.

 Similarly, when you are with someone you've recently started dating, and experience a too strong to ignore flutter in your heart, it could be an indication of having found the person who'd like to spend the rest of your life with. Our body is constantly trying to communicate emotions we may not be aware of through physical sensations. Listening to these feelings and emotions signaled by the body helps process our emotions and reactions more efficiently.

Tap Into Your Subconscious Mind

How can you gain a greater awareness of your subconscious emotions or feelings? Apart from deep breathing and mindfulness, let your thoughts wander freely and evaluate where they go. Pay close attention to your dreams. Are there any recurring symbols that can be closely connected with the current events in your life?

Keep a journal and pen next to your bed and write down the details you can recall about your most compelling dreams as soon as you are up. Analyze the emotions and patterns of these dreams, their symbolic references and the message they are trying to communicate. When you gain a thorough understanding of the emotions that dominate your subconscious mind, it becomes simpler to train your subconscious mind to guide your actions.

Sometimes, our conscious minds are unable to come with solutions we are faced with, which is why the phrase "sleep over it" originated. Our subconscious mind's functionality is at its peak when we are asleep. Ever wondered why many a times the solution to our problems strikes us when we are asleep? Or we wake up with a totally different perspective or solution much to our surprise? Our subconscious mind is ticking overtime when our conscious mind is resting. By tuning into our subconscious mind, we are tapping into our inner most emotional reserve to uncover our deepest feelings.

Boost Your Social EQ with These Powerful Verbal and Non-Verbal Clues

We've established in earlier how emotional intelligence is the master key to effective leadership and social skills. By tuning into other people's emotions or by empathizing with how they feel, there is a higher chance that you will respond appropriately to create the desired positive result. Thus, our ability to connect with our own and other people's emotions can be a powerful tool in social and leadership situations.

Understanding other people, helping overcome stress situations, motivating your team, negotiating business deals, and building a close-knit social circle becomes easier when you can use the emotional information you have about them as leverage. It increases situational awareness and our ability to read people, thus helping us make the most positive decision.

Here are some verbal and non-verbal factors impacting social-emotional quotient, or our ability to read and deal with people:

Verbal clues

A person's choice of words can say a lot about what they are thinking and feeling. Words are symbolic of our thoughts and feelings which, when combined with non-verbal clues, give us a comprehensive understanding of their emotional state.

The human brain is a miracle, really. When we think, or process rational and logical thoughts, we tend to use nouns and verbs. Conversely, when we attempt to express our thoughts or feelings in a verbal or written format, there is a tendency to use more adverbs and adjectives.

Any basic sentence features a subject and a verb. For example, "I walked." When a person adds more words to it, they can indicate their feelings or personality. For example, "I walked fast," can indicate a sense of urgency, fear, or insecurity. There are clear reasons why people use specific words over others.

Similarly, there is a hidden meaning behind what people say. Through their choice of words, people reveal emotions left unsaid.

Let's say you booked a table to take your family out for dinner at one of the fanciest, fine dining restaurants that recently opened in your neighborhood. The server greets you courteously and directs you to your table. What follows is an amazing dining experience.

The waiter introduces each of the seven courses in an informative yet engaging style, while you dine and enjoy wine in an upscale ambiance. After you enjoy a hearty meal and call for the tab, the waiter inquires if you enjoyed the food. You reply with, "The entrées were good."

The waiter doesn't look very delighted, even if what you said is a compliment in your opinion. Those four words you uttered reveal your real opinion about the food. It implies that other than the entrées, everything else was pretty average or the only thing that stood out during the entire meal were the entrées.

Did you actually say everything else other than the entrées was average? No. Then why did the waiter look crestfallen at your statement? It is obvious, people convey a lot not only through what they say but also through what they leave unsaid. Gather the hidden meaning or subtext behind what people say to tune in to their inner feelings. Notice how sometimes people will say, "You look very lovely today." It can either mean you look plain every day (which is a more passive-aggressive kind of statement), or you are looking exceptionally good today compared to other days.

Another powerful clue about what people are thinking or feeling is noticing how they talk about other people. In a research published in the Journal of Personality and Social Psychology, headed by Peter Harms and Simine Vazire of the University of Nebraska and University of St. Louis respectively, it was discovered that merely asking participants to rate positive and negative traits of three other people revealed a lot about the participants' social competence, general well-being, other people's perception of them, and their mental health.

It was observed that an individual's inclination to view other people in a positive manner was a strong indication of their own positive emotions. There is a strong link between seeing others in a more positive light and being emotionally stable, happy, productive, and enthusiastic.

On the other hand, viewing others in a negative light bears a strong correlation with a general sense of dissatisfaction, low self-esteem, anti-social behavior, and narcissism. People who hold plenty of negative emotions tend to perceive other people in a poorer or more negative light. This can also be an indication of emotional issues, mental health conditions, or a personality disorder. Again, emotions aren't good or bad but are reflections of how you are feeling. If a person experiences more negative emotions for others around them, it can be a clue to how they really feel about themselves.

If a person says that they 'made up their mind' after plenty of deliberation, the phrase indicates a mindset that is high on logic and rational thinking. The individual may be more contemplative and practical by nature. He or she may consider all the available options before making a decision. These are not your likely contenders for a snap of the moment decisions.

Do you know what metalanguage is? It is the intended words behind the words you speak. You don't say something directly but reveal it through the words you use. For example, notice how when people want to get someone to agree with what they've said, they'll always place yes, done, or okay followed by a question mark at the end. For example, "I can't hand in the project today. I'll submit it tomorrow, okay?" It is like manipulating the other person to agree.

To further increase your social-emotional quotient, pay attention to the sounds people utter, other than coherent words. Moaning, grunting, sighing, etc. can reveal a lot. Sometimes, these sounds will complement the words the speaker is using to make the message even more persuasive. However, at other times, there may be a mismatch between the person's words and sounds.

For example, someone may say, "I am having a really good day," followed by a sigh, which can indicate they are simply being sarcastic and are in fact having a bad day. You can even understand more about what a person really means when you observe their words and other miscellaneous sounds they make.

Environmental clues

A person's immediate environment says a lot about their emotional state. For instance, a messy, unclean, or disorganized space can indicate a lack of clarity of emotions or thoughts. Of course, everything has to be analyzed within a context. Someone may have an unkempt house because he or she is too busy to tidy it up and doesn't have housekeeping help.

All of us have certain spaces around us that are inaccessible that we don't really bother cleaning or organizing (space behind the cupboard or under the bed). These are spaces that we wouldn't normally clean. If such spaces are immaculately clean or organized, it can indicate anxiety or a disorder (obsessive-compulsive disorder).

Well-organized and clean spaces can indicate clarity of emotions or control over one's emotions. The person tends to be more reflective and introverted by nature. Similarly, people who are outwardly focused, or extroverts, tend to be surrounded by chaos.

This isn't pop psychology, but it is based on clear principles of how the environment around us is created through our actions, which themselves are directed by our subconscious thoughts and emotions. For example, using bright, vibrant, and bold prints in your décor or attire can be a sign of confidence, emotional self-assurance, and independence of thought or opinion. Likewise, a home with brighter and more vibrant colors is an indication of being bold, emotionally expressive, and outgoing. These people are not afraid of taking risks and are more than capable of understanding the needs and feelings of other people. More subtle colors imply inward directed emotions, or an introverted personality. These people may not be too receptive to another person's feelings and emotions.

People who hold on to old objects or hoard various objects can be excessively emotional, sensitive, or sentimental. They find it tough to move away from their past emotions or are still ridden by feelings of shame, regret, and guilt related to the past. These are people who latch on to old memories and can't release the emotions that hold them back.

When you use these verbal and non-verbal principles to understand people, your social-emotional quotient invariably increases.

Tone

The tone, volume, pitch, and emphasis of a person's voice can help you decode the hints that can help you tell what they are feeling. For example, if you notice plenty of inconsistencies in the tone of their voice as they speak, they are probably very angry, hurt, excited, or nervous. Ever notice how your voice shakes when you speak in a rage or are nervous about something? It can also be a sign the person is lying.

Similarly, if a person is speaking louder or softer than their regular volume, something may be amiss. Again, a person's tone is a dead giveaway. Sometimes people say something that sounds like a compliment. However, upon examining their tone closely, you realize the sarcasm and the condescension with which it was uttered.

The tone in which an individual ends their sentence says a lot about what they are trying to convey even with similar verbal clues. For example, if a person completes their sentence on a raised note, they are doubtful of something or are asking a question. Similarly, if they finish the sentence with a flat tone, they are pronouncing a statement or judgment. Watch out for how people end their sentences to get a clue about their inner feelings.

Again, the words people emphasize can help you uncover their true feelings. For example, if a person says, "Have you borrowed the blazer?" while emphasizing 'borrowed,' it indicates their doubt over whether you have borrowed, stolen, or done something else to the blazer. However, if the emphasis is on 'you,' they aren't sure if it is you or someone else who has borrowed the blazer.

I also like to look at pauses between phrases to know about the person's attitude, emotions, and intentions. For example, if a person pauses after saying something, it could be because what they just said is extremely important to them, or they truly believe in it. Sometimes, a person pauses to seek validation or feedback from others. The speaker wants to gauge your reaction to what they said since it is important for them.

When people are in a more emotionally unstable or negative frame of mind (angry, hurt, or upset), their voice tends to be higher pitched or squeaky. They are most likely losing a grip on their emotions or aren't able to regulate their emotions effectively. Notice how, when people are very angry, their voice becomes more screechy and squeaky, as if they are about to cry.

The speed of a speech

A person's emotions clearly impact the speed of their speech. Notice how you start talking much faster than your normal rate of speech, or words per minute, when you are angry or upset. A rapid speech can convey lack of organization, uncertainty, or lack of clarity. The person is not very comfortable with speaking and is just trying to finish throwing his or her words. Again, a slower than usual pace translates into low self-confidence, inability to express emotions, inability to come to terms with one's emotions, lack of emotional reassurance, and other similar feelings.

Body language

Research reveals that body language accounts for 50 percent of our communication. You'd wonder why there were words in the first place if body language accounts for half the communication process. Tuning in to a person's body language will help you pick up important signals related to their emotional state and subconscious thoughts or feelings.

Here's a quick cue sheet to reading people's feelings through their body language:

•   Crossed arms and legs are signals of people creating a subconscious barrier. They are emotionally closed, suspicious, or do not subscribe to your ideas. They aren't open to listening to your views or are disinterested in the topic of conversation. You may have to emotionally open the person up a bit by changing the topic and then get back to the original topic. The physical act of uncrossing their arms and legs will make them more subconsciously receptive to your ideas.

•   How can you tell a genuine smile from a fake one? Simple, it's all in the eyes. Observe that there's crinkled skin near the person's eyes forming crow's feet. People often present a happy expression to hide their true feelings. However, if their smile doesn't cause the skin around their eyes and mouth to crinkle, they are most likely not as happy as they are pretending to be. Artificial smiles create wrinkles only around the mouth, while genuine smiles create wrinkles around the sides of the eyes.

•   When people constantly take their gaze away from you while speaking, they are most likely not being very honest or trying to hide something. Similarly, if a person speaks to you without taking their gaze away from you for long, they may be trying to threaten or intimidate you with their gaze. It is alright to look away periodically. However, shifting gaze constantly is a red flag.

•   When you are addressing a group of people, closely observe the ones who are nodding excessively or in a more exaggerated manner. These are the people who are most concerned about your approval. They are anxious about making a positive impression and want to be in your 'good books.'

• People who are nervous or anxious tend to fidget with their hands or objects. Other signs of nervousness also include excessive blinking, tapping feet, and constantly running one's hand over the face.

• When an entire group walks into the room, how do you analyze who the leader or decision maker is? Quickly observe everyone's posture. The leader will most likely walk with a straight posture, with shoulders pulled out. Subconsciously, they are trying to occupy maximum space to convey authority over their team. Standing straight and pulling back shoulders increases a person's physical frame. It makes them come across as much bigger than they actually are. This is why people in power love to keep this posture to show their influence over a group or place.

• Expressions are the windows into a person's emotional state. When a person is amazed or surprised, their eyebrows are raised, and the upper eyelids widen. Similarly, the mouth gapes open. Expressions can often overlap, so watch for micro expressions that can reveal precise emotions.

• For instance, raised eyebrows can also reveal fear. Look for other micro expression clues to determine the exact emotion. If a person is experiencing fear, the eyebrows will be raised and pulled together with tensed lower eyelids, while the two corners of their lips will appear stretched. Similarly, a person's surprise is expressed by eyebrows pulled up and a lowered jaw. Learn to read the entire face, especially micro expressions, if you want to learn more about how a person is feeling.

•   Since micro expressions occur in fractions of seconds, they are virtually impossible to fake. For instance, notice how when people are being deceptive, their mouths will slightly angle differently. Similarly, their eye movements become more rapid, the nostrils flare a little bit, and they purse their lips together (a subconscious gesture signaling their lips are sealed, or they won't reveal the truth). Since these split expressions are driven by the subconscious, this makes them involuntary, and it is almost impossible to manipulate them.

•   Enlarged pupils reveal intense emotions such as excitement, elation, delight, surprise, and interest. When a person is attracted to you or truly delighted to see you, their pupils will involuntarily enlarge.

•   The direction of a person's feet can also determine what's going on in their mind. Since feet aren't the first thing on anyone's mind, it's harder to manipulate body language related to legs and feet. If a person's feet are pointing away from you, they are subconsciously signaling their need to escape. However, if their feet are pointed towards you, they are interested or in agreement with what you are saying.

•   Typical signs of frustration and stress are clenched jaws, wrinkled eyebrows, and tensed neck. The person's words notwithstanding, if you observe any of these signs, he or she may be undergoing a stressful situation that they are trying to conceal. The trick for reading people's emotions accurately is to keep an eye out for a clear mismatch between verbal and non-verbal clues.

•   Observe a person's walk to tune in to their feelings. People with a heavier gait along with low gravity while moving their legs are most likely hurt, stressed, frustrated, or depressed. People who walk with a slower and more relaxed pace are reflecting upon something. Notice how confident, happy, and goal-oriented people walk swiftly in one direction.

•   Observing a person's eye movements is a near accurate way of gauging how he or she is feeling since our eye movements are connected to precise brain functions. Our eye movements have an established pattern depending on the brain function or type of information we are trying to access. For example, when a person is caught in an internal conflict or dilemma (to speak the truth or lie), they are more likely to look in the direction of their left collarbone. Darting sideways from one side to another can be a red flag that indicates deception.

•   Proxemics is a subtopic within body language that talks about how people reveal their feelings and emotions through the physical distance they maintain with other people during the process of face-to-face interaction or communication. It is a very useful non-verbal signal for understanding a person's thought process or state of mind.

Psychologists and body language experts believe that the amount of physical distance we maintain while interacting with a person helps establish the dynamics of our relationship with them or reveals our emotions about them.

A person who isn't standing very close to you may not be emotionally open or receptive to you. They may have a tendency to closely guard their emotions or give only a little of themselves to the interaction. Such people may be more emotionally guarded and closed. You may need to make extra effort to get them to drop their guard and feel less intimidated. It may be a defense mechanism against being emotionally hurt or vulnerable.

On the other hand, if a person is leaning in your direction, they may subconsciously convey being emotionally open, or they trust you with their feelings. They may also be more interested in what you are speaking about.

Secrets of Building Healthy Social Relationships

Yes, when you listen keenly to people, empathize with them, and try to understand things from their perspective, it paves the way for healthier and more rewarding relationships. We must understand that emotional intelligence is not a static skill that we acquire and will last a lifetime. It is a lifelong process and skill that keeps evolving as we navigate various relationships. However, there are a few established tips that will help you sharpen your emotional skills and help you relate to other people more effectively, thus helping you build strong relationships. Here are a few tips for using the power of emotional intelligence to build healthy relationships:

Avoid Complaining

Complaining is a huge sign of low emotional intelligence. It happens when a person believes he is victimized and that the situation is beyond his or her control. They will pass on the blame to the next person or situation before thinking it through.

Emotionally intelligent people think in a constructive manner to resolve the issue rather than blaming someone else or complaining. They operate from a mindset that seeks to resolve the problem rather than working from the perspective of just making complaints.

Complaining is a huge sign that people believe they are mere victims of a situation and that the solution is beyond their reach. We consider ourselves victims of other people or circumstances and therefore are unable to find solutions to pressing issues. We believe that the solutions to the circumstances enveloping us are beyond our realm of control. An emotionally intelligent person seldom believes himself or herself to be a victim. They rarely feel that problem resolution is beyond their control. In place of blaming something or someone, they approach the matter in a more constructive manner and look for a solution quietly.

Emotionally intelligent folks will peacefully contemplate an issue and look for a resolution through reflection and consideration of all possibilities in lieu of the current circumstances. There is a sense of maturity in their thinking and manner of approach.

The next time you are tempted to blame your alarm clock for waking up late and showing up late at work, resist the urge and focus on what you can do to wake up on time each morning. Can you cut down on post work partying? Can you watch less television and go to bed early instead? Can you set the alarm on two clocks, so you have a back-up if one conks out? There are many ways to resolve the issue if you get out of the victim zone and start looking for proactive solutions that are within your control.

Sonja Lyubomirsky's research has suggested that 50 percent of our happy state of mind is influenced by factors that are beyond control (genes, personality, temperament). The other 50 percent is influenced by a combination of multiple factors such as attitude (over which we have full control). Practice celebrating joy even in the most seemingly adverse situation.

Open Yourself Up to Establish a Connection

One of the fastest and most surefire ways to build a connection with people is to listen to their experiences with empathy and link it with a similar experience you've undergone. This exchange of similar experiences strikes the right chord in people and makes them open up to you. Don't be afraid to open up a bit and share a similar experience when the other person is sharing theirs. For instance, someone may talk about how painful it has been to grow up in a single parent home. You may be tempted not to share that information about yourself too early on or open up before knowing the person really well, but it can help establish a connection. You can add how you completely understand how it feels because you had been living in a single parent home all through your teens. This is a quick way to set the foundation for a lasting relationship.

Develop a sense of curiosity when it comes to strangers. Emotionally intelligent folks are intrigued by strangers and always have an insatiable hunger to know more about them and understand their lives and views. They make an attempt to understand how the opinions and perspectives of these people are different from theirs. You know what to do next time you're on the train or at the airport. Immerse yourself in a different culture by traveling to various destinations whenever you can. It broadens your understanding of people and cultures. Sometimes, the only way to have an open mind is to go to a different destination and establish connections with locals.

Focus on How You Say it

What you say is important, but how you convey it is even more vital. There are multiple ways to say the same thing or handle a situation. Non-verbal communication can have a massive impact on how you are perceived by people.

Eye contact, voice, tone, expressions, and body language all contribute towards creating an impression about you among other people. It conveys to others how you are thinking and feeling emotionally. Think whether your body language and emotions complement each other. Are you able to articulate your emotions or feelings without offending the other person?

Keep in mind that few things destroy an individual's morale quicker than an overly critical person. Think of different ways to say something without affecting the other person negatively. I always recommend learning something about the other person or understanding them before attempting to communicate with them. For instance, if someone is particularly sensitive, they may not appreciate a direct, straightforward approach. You may have to get your point across in a more diplomatic and tactful manner.

Similarly, straightforward folks may not appreciate you beating around the bush. You may also have to employ a more frank and forthright approach. Thus, knowing an individual's personality will help you communicate with him or her in a more effective manner.

How you say it makes all the difference while communicating, especially on slightly tricky topics. For example, let's take a scenario where you think an employee is not suitable for a specific department and has consistently underperformed there despite receiving the best training, development, and mentoring.

As a manager, it is your responsibility to inform him that he or she is going to be shifted to another department. Now you are placed with the conundrum of telling them the truth without affecting his or her morale. What approach would you take as an emotionally intelligent person to accomplish the same?

Instead of telling the person that he or she isn't good in 'XYZ' department and that he or she is being shifted to another department, you can focus on the positive of the situation and change the angle or approach to give it a more positive twist. You can say something like, "We think you have the ideal skills for (new department) and that your skills or qualities will be utilized to the fullest there." You are still telling the employee that he or she will be transferred to another department, but you are putting across your point in a manner that doesn't offend them or lower their morale. You are simply telling him or her that their skills aren't being utilized to the fullest in the current department instead of telling him or her that their skills are not good enough for the current department. The words, body language, and approach make all the difference.

Also, active listening is a huge component of emotional intelligence, especially during conflicts. Often, while arguing with people, we have our responses ready even before the other person finishes speaking.

During heated discussions, arguments, and conflicts, we only listen to reply but not to understand the other person. How many times have you heard the other person out to truly understand them and not to prepare your response to what he or she is saying? Resist the urge to come across as too overpowering during a disagreement and try to understand where the other person is coming from. Deal with issues in a respective, productive, and assertive manner, without an element of defensiveness. When you actively and empathetically listen to the other person, you are also creating a space for your feelings and emotions to be heard. When you listen intently to the other person's views, you drain all the toxic energy from the situation and instead focus on arriving at a beneficial solution.

I always recommend practicing your non-verbal skills at home to make yourself even more clear and transparent in social situations. Start at your home because it is a space that doesn't make you feel overwhelmed, unlike an alien setting. Make a video of yourself interacting with a friend or relative.

Watch it so you can know what areas you can improve in when it comes to non-verbal signals. Another super way is to practice before a mirror. Pretend that you are interacting with a person and watch yourself in the mirror. Enlist the help of trusted folks when it comes to gaining valuable feedback. They can offer helpful insights about your voice, posture, expressions, and more. You'll be in a more private, low-stress setting, which reduces your shyness and preps your confidence for more important interactions. It's actually enjoyable to try out multiple gestures, expressions, signs, and postures.

When you can read non-verbal signals passed by others, you can quickly spot the disagreement in their feelings or emotions and words. Even a subtle mismatch in verbal and non-verbal signals will help you understand the other person's feelings and behavior.

Notice how sometimes you pick up some clue and call it a "hunch" that something isn't right about what the person is saying. What we like to call or think of as a gut feeling, or hunch, is actually a subconscious notice of the mismatch between the person's body language and words. The person didn't intend to communicate it, but we tuned in to their body language and "listened" to it.

Spend Time Away from the Social Media

Though this is the age of the social media, try and balance your online time and connections with offline relationships too. It is important to maintain face to face relationships with people since it paves the way for developing better social skills. Don't go messaging people. Instead, meet them over dinner or drinks and have a real, face to face conversation. Emotional intelligence goes beyond social media confines and needs real-world connections. Our ability to identify, process, and manage emotions is impeded by instant messaging and social media. Emoticons don't build emotional intelligence. It expands when we actually get out there and interact with people face to face. Staying in the constricted space of social media doesn't allow you to experience real emotions that can increase your emotional perception and intelligence.

Isolate One Skill

If you are looking to improve emotional intelligence and social skills, rather than trying to be good at everything, isolate one skill that you want to develop at a time. For instance, you may want to work on your listening skills or develop greater empathy. Don't try to work on too many aspects at a time. Identify one component of social-emotional intelligence and observe someone who is particularly good at it. If you know a friend is really good at listening to people and making them feel comfortable, try and observe how they manage their emotions, react, and speak. How does their body language reveal that they are keenly listening to the other person? How do they acknowledge what the other person is saying? What are the usual words they use to make the person feel comfortable? This technique has been suggested by none other than the father of the term "Emotional Intelligence," Daniel Goleman himself.

Reduce Stress and Practice Staying More Lighthearted

Stress rears its ugly head in all ways of life and completely consumes us following a range of negative emotions. From relationship breakdowns to being laid off from work, there are plenty of emotions that can overwhelm us. When you are stressed, it is challenging to behave reasonably. It will be tough to be emotionally intelligent when you are under tremendous stress.

Find what your stress triggers are and make a list of everything you can do to relieve yourself of that stress. What is it that helps decrease your stress? A long lonesome walk in the midst of nature? Listening to soothing music? Talking to a trusted friend? Having lunch at your favorite café?

Enlist the help of a professional therapist if it feels too overpowering to handle it by yourself. A psychologist, counselor, or therapist can help you cope with the stress in an effective and professional manner, while also helping you raise your emotional quotient. It is easier to establish rewarding interpersonal relationships with people when you are not under stress.

I personally love to combat stress by maintaining a lighthearted atmosphere at work, home, and other social scenarios. It is simpler to appreciate the joy and beauty of life when you take on a more humorous or lighthearted approach. It makes others around you feel less stressed too. Optimism and positivity not just lead to better emotional health (for yourself and others) but also more opportunities. (Who doesn't like being around a positive and optimistic person?) People are naturally drawn to optimistic, lighthearted, and positive people. Negativity, on the other hand, builds defenses. People with high emotional quotient use lots of fun, jokes, and humor to make the atmosphere for others (and themselves) safe, joyful, and happy. Laughter is indeed the best medicine to get through challenging times in our life.

Practice Assertiveness and Expressing Challenging Emotions

An essential part of being who you really are is asserting or being able to speak frankly and openly about things that truly matter to you or are important in your life. Practice taking a clear position on where you stand when it comes to vital emotional issues. Draw clear lines about what is acceptable and not acceptable in relationships.

Setting boundaries in relationships is also a huge component of emotional intelligence. It isn't restricted to being empathetic and being nice to others. Emotional intelligence is also about being fair to yourself.

Set clear boundaries so others can know more about your position which leads to lesser misunderstandings in relationships. This can include anything from disagreeing with someone about establishing priorities, to saying no, to protecting yourself from physical harm or mental duress.

Use the "I feel...when you" technique to assert yourself in tricky situations. For instance, "I strongly feel that I deserve a promotion from the organization based on my performance and contribution."

Similarly, when you are not comfortable doing something for someone over your own priorities you can assert yourself saying something like, "I don't feel comfortable that you expect me to do everything for you over my tasks and priorities." When you feel disappointed that someone doesn't follow through or listen to your instructions, you can articulate it with something like, "I feel really upset or disappointed that you didn't update me about the project despite being instructed to do so."

The trick is to say how you feel when something happens. Refrain from beginning your sentence with "you." It makes you sound accusatory and judgment. The moment the other person hears "you," he or she will subconsciously slip into a defensive position. You are quickly allowing the listener to assume a defensive position, followed by a bunch of excuses. If you want people to listen to you, talk about how you feel when they do something.

Learning not to Judge

During the course of our lives, we tend to judge people because we have a set of standards and these are imposed upon us by our parents and upon them by their parents. Then there are standards set by peers and the standards of society in general. The problem with measuring everything by these standards is that it limits who you are because you are not making a decision based on something that has any solidity. You are basing it upon unwritten rules and that's not a very emotionally intelligent thing to do.

If you want to learn to use your emotional intelligence, you need to be able to let go of judgment and one of the best ways to do this is to learn to meditate. The process of meditation hones in on learning how to let go of thoughts or to see them and not judge them and it's a hard lesson to learn. If you take lessons in meditation or learn to do it yourself, you will find that the mind slows down a little and that when things are said that you would normally judge, you tend to step back a bit from them and don't judge. You simply use the information and quietly deduct whatever you need to in order to help the situation, rather than add complexity to it.

The first place to start is learning to breathe correctly, in through the nostrils and out to a counting system. You count eight as you breathe in and then as you breathe out and as thoughts come to you, you acknowledge them and then dismiss them. They are not appropriate at the time when you are meditating, so you learn to be able to let go of them. If you practice even for as little as fifteen minutes a day, every day, you find that you are not one that judges situations too hastily and this also helps to calm down the emotions and be able to solve things without going through all the negative feelings that people who judge have to endure.

Try it and I am sure that you will find this to be so. Every time that you pass judgment on something, what you are doing is putting up barriers. These barriers make you biased and biased people don't have much emotional intelligence at all. They are too busy building barriers against the world that doesn't fit in with their ideals. The tramp on the corner of the street may just have something valid to say. Don't ignore him because he is a tramp. The preacher in a church may just say something that helps you to see the end to a problem. Even if you are a non-believer, don't put up walls without waiting to hear what is being said. Whenever you do this, you make your emotions snap into judgment mode and that's the unhealthiest state of your mind.

I remember being told that one particular child in a class was trouble. The fact was that the teacher passing this information on wasn't very emotionally intelligent. What the truth of the situation was, as it came to light later, was that she didn't have the teaching abilities to deal with this particular child's problems. Usually, when the pieces don't go together right during the course of your lifetime, there is another reason other than blame and blame doesn't help anyone.

Emotionally intelligent people will be the first to forgive others because they know that circumstances differ for everyone and there may have been reasons why someone did what they did. The world at large is much bigger than what goes on in your head and emotionally intelligent people know this. The reason I suggested meditation as the first step toward emotional intelligence is that it helps you to see things in perspective, slows down your anger and negative feelings and helps you to be able to assess each individual situation using something people don't seem to use much anymore – intuition. When you unlock your intuition, you can trust it because it is there to safeguard you and it helps you to be able to see beyond the obvious.

People who have a high level of emotional intelligence will be calm people who are not quick to judge others, who are able to forgive easily and who understand that their own actions actually dictate the outcome of a situation. They tend not to blame others but instead look into themselves to see what could be done to improve any given situation. That's the difference between them and ordinary people whose level of emotional intelligence is low.

Learning to Gain Confidence

If you want to gain confidence, emotional intelligence will help you to achieve this. Instead of feeling unsure of your actions and hesitating, hesitate for the right reasons. This hesitation is simply your way of being more certain that the response you give will be one that is considered. Learn to look at your face in the mirror and ask yourself questions that you fear answering. Then, look at the facial expressions that you use when these questions are posed.

The changes in your facial body language come because your emotions kick in whether you want them to or not. Ask people around you questions and you will be able to recognize doubt, lying, unhappiness and all kinds of emotional responses, but that's something that can help you. As you gain confidence in recognizing these things, by using your intuition, you actually start to understand your own reactions better and are able to stem those actions that let you down.

Mary was always upset about the way that people treated her as if she was incompetent. However, when she did this exercise, she suddenly realized that her own reactions were what fueled this opinion in people and she was able to change that. When your emotions turn to confusion or anger, you have a habit of changing your facial expression and your body language. Try it again with the use of a mirror. Shock yourself if you have to because all of this trains you to respond in a different way. When Mary stopped looking in a blank way at people giving her instructions, they started to trust her more with the tasks that they had given her. She was able to develop trusting relationships as well because people didn't know what to make of her expressions and she could see clearly in the mirror what was causing all of this negativity in people who communicated with her.

In fact, you can also make a mental note of times when responses have not been the way you wanted them to be and note down what the questions were and what the responses were so that you are better able to analyze reactions and adjust the way that you put yourself over as a communicator. Look at people who communicate well and who appear to have confidence and their body language is what you need to aim for. The head back, the smile, the shoulders back and the confident stride all help you to be seen as different by others, but they also help you to use your emotional intelligence in a more effective way.

It may be worthwhile keeping a journal. Before you go to bed every night, write out your worries or your doubts and try to come to some kind of conclusion about how you will face them with a smile or at least in a positive way. The things that get in the way of emotional intelligence are:

- Negative thoughts

- Negative self-talk

- Negative emotions

You can look at your own behavior over a given period and try to change your way of handling situations. Instead of negative thoughts, replace them with positive ones. Instead of negative self-talk, start to praise the things that you know you can do well and gradually improve upon the things you find difficult. That feeling that a cyclist gets when he/she first learns to balance on a bike is unforgettable because it's so positive and if you can convert your life into a series of events that all have positive outcomes, you will feel that buzz and people around you will also pick up on your positive energy.

When you find that you are talking negatively to yourself, replace that thought as soon as it comes with breathing exercises that bring you into the moment because these help you to move forward and to realize that you have this habit of talking negatively to yourself. You can even have a song that you can sing quietly in your mind to get rid of these negative thoughts. Emotional intelligence immediately recognizes when a positive input is needed and that's what you are aiming for.

Try and be more empathetic as well. This means being able to place yourself in the shoes of someone else. Instead of thinking negative things about others, try to understand where the negativity or emotional reaction they give comes from and you will find empathy will help you to feel better about them and also about yourself. This helps you to gain confidence and to feel better about being you. Give a beggar a sandwich or try to imagine what it's like for the homeless and do something voluntarily with absolutely no strings attached because when you do, you show your emotional intelligence and will find that voluntary actions actually fuel confidence in yourself.

Learning to Listen to your Body and Learn to Listen to Others

Although the above quotation relates to talking with someone else, it also applies equally when you talk to yourself. Often you don't listen sufficiently to give reasonable answers and that's where emotional intelligence comes in. When you learn to listen to your body, this means that you are able to slow your life down a little and remember the importance of being aware of how you feel. If you were to stop people in the street and ask how they feel, chances are most people would shrug the question off and ask what you mean. The fact is that there are clues in the messages we receive from our bodies that help us to feel better or to feel more positive, but often we throw the answers at them before we have actually taken the time to be logical and to examine why the body is sending those messages in the first place.

Let me try to examine this in detail so that you can see the sequence of events. If your neck hurts, you may start to feel irritable. You may even shake your head to try to get rid of the ache or swallow a pill hoping that the neck ache will simply vanish. An emotionally intelligent person doesn't tend to do either. They take the time to listen to their body and are able to distinguish from the symptoms what they need to do to ease the pain. Perhaps posture hasn't helped. Perhaps the ache is as a result of sitting in the same position over an extended period. When you don't listen to your body and your aches persist, what happens is that you begin to feel worse and that eventually changes your humor and your emotional wellbeing.

However, if you examine why your body is sending the messages, you can do something tangible about it, so that the body doesn't have to send those messages anymore. For example:

• Change your posture to avoid the pain

• Change your seat, so you don't suffer any more

• Work out what's going on with your body and do something to relieve the pain

Negative people tend to rely on the messages from their body to justify their negativity. However, motivated people with a good sense of emotional intelligence don't do this. They simply work out the problem and do not allow the messages from the body to turn into negative messages that make them feel worse. There's absolutely no benefit to feeling negative about your neck ache. When you feel negative, your emotions jump in and you are snappy and not very nice to be with. When you allow emotional intelligence to step in, you find solutions and thus never reach the point where emotions are able to take over.

It's very much the same when you are listening to people. Really listen. Don't cut into the conversation and assume that what you have to say has more credence than that said by others. When you do, you miss opportunities to get to know people and to learn things. People who do this think very highly of themselves and think their opinions are more important than the opinions of people they are listening to. This makes them emotionally draining. Have you ever met someone who does this? You may know the know-it-all character that visits you and who doesn't listen to anything that you have to say. Do you want people to see you in that way? If not, the only way out of a situation like this is to be patient. Listen with all of your attention. Breathe before you reply. Think out your answers and bear in mind that others are entitled to have different views.

Emotionally intelligent people are those who are open to learning. They not only listen to their own bodies, but they listen to other people and make those around them feel like they are important or liked. That's a very important element because when you stop feeling that way, you actually alienate people and can find that your emotional lows are as a result of your own actions, rather than of the actions of others. Listening to kids can really help you to learn to use your emotional intelligence. Sometimes they come out with amazingly astute ideas that maybe you have left behind you as you have grown up. Embrace the child inside sometimes because we are all entitled to. Those who are able to do this have great imaginations, can see others' points of view and also know that the reason their bodies are complaining is because there is just cause. Emotionally intelligent people find the cause and work on it so that they have a more enriching experience in the future.

If you are not prepared to listen, you will learn nothing at all and your emotional intelligence will be stunted. Hear the laughter of children. Feel the magical feeling of emotional freedom and enjoy experiencing that laughter with someone else who needs it and you will find that your emotional intelligence quota will improve.

Chapter 4: Connecting The Dots

There are times in your life when you feel bad about life or when your emotions go into overdrive. This is quite normal as long as you don't let the emotions dictate the outcome. People who are emotionally intelligent are able to look back at situations that provoked the same kind of emotional response. When they do that, they are also able to see that it was only a matter of time and circumstance that took them out of those negative emotions and back on track. People without emotional intelligence are unable to do that.

For example, if you are drawn to tears of frustration when things go wrong, your mind will analyze the situation and you can join up the dots. You may be saying to yourself that the last time you felt that bad, you managed to move forward by being patient and seeing what the outcome was, rather than assuming the worst. The problem is that people in an emotional state of mind often don't bother to look back and see similar situations where things were solved. They are too busy being unhappy. The emotionally intelligent person knows for example that frustration of this kind triggers an emotional response. They, therefore, understand where the emotional inadequacy comes from and can rationalize it.

The next time that you feel emotional, instead of acting on that emotion, try to analyze it. If you can remember the last time that you felt that way and look at what the outcome was, this helps you to remain focused even though your emotions are trying to take over. Don't let them. You are the driver and when you analyze these things, you make better sense of them. Let me demonstrate.

Kate felt an overwhelming sense of being out of control and was feeling tears running down her cheeks. She could have become even more emotional but chose not to. Instead, she looked at her current circumstances and then looked back to another time in her life when she had felt that bad and was able to see quite clearly that there was a reason for the emotional response. She was then able to calm herself knowing that this response was normal and that there was nothing wrong with her or that response. When you can rationalize your response, it doesn't do as much harm because you don't take it out on the first person that comes along. Instead of doing that, you look inwardly and find your own conclusions.

If you find that you are emotional, try to spend a little more time alone and analyze your feelings and work out why they are happening. The elements to keep out of the picture are:

- Blame

- Jealousy

- Hate

- Anger

These all taint your results. For example, Kate could have blamed her coworker for the way that she was feeling. She could have said that her coworker was throwing too much work at her, but that wasn't, in fact, the case. Although, to an outsider, it may have looked that way, what Kate was actually crying about was that things at home were not the way that she wanted them to be. When she separated these facts from work facts, she was able to get back on track and then tackle the home situation with a fresh outlook, which helped it rather than aggravate it. Someone with less emotional intelligence may have spent the day grumbling about her husband and tried to get people within the office to take sides with her. All this does is fuel a fire and that fire may not actually be necessary. Don't use others to stoke your fires. When you do, things get out of control and your situation becomes worse, rather than better.

If you analyze your feelings, you can then walk away from them because you are able to give them a name or put logic into the situation that doesn't involve others, but merely examines the thoughts and emotions that you have going on in your head and recognizes these from past events. You will then take control of your emotions, knowing and trusting that these negative feelings will pass and that the problem is not as large as your emotional mind is making it out to be.

The Chain of Goals and Intentions

Here's how you can differently use the Chain of Goals technique not only to solve your internal conflicts, but also to work on many other things. It could be your procrastination, getting angry in certain situations, your laziness and stress recurring at specific times or fear of meeting new people. It must be something that is inside you, something about which you have an internal representation. Don't work on things and issues that are dependent on other people.

You can also pick something that is not a problem per-se, but needs to be improved. It could be motivation to do something, being more passionate about your project, waking up early, etc. The choice is yours.

Specify the thing you want to work on in one sentence as a concrete action or behavior (e.g. "I'm always getting angry when...I always procrastinate when...I'm stressed out in situations like..." etc.). Then take these steps:

1. Imagine a situation in which the problem or behavior specified by you takes place. Take a moment to relax and visualize this situation.

2. Think about a part of your body in which this piece of you being responsible for this action or behavior resides. Locate this spot.

3. Turn to this spot in your body where this part of yourself is and ask it, "What do you want? What precisely do you want to achieve by doing that?" Wait for the answer and then write it down on a piece of paper. This answer is your first intention. Say "thank you" to this part for giving you the answer.

4. Now, feel how it is when this new intention is entirely fulfilled, when you have fully obtained what this part of you wants to accomplish by this initial behavior/action you're

working on. Do as much as you can to feel it deeply and ask yourself this question, "Once you have and fully feel (intention number 1 or further intentions) what you want to achieve by doing what you are usually doing, what's even more important now?" Wait for the answer and write it down. This is the next intention.

5. Create your chain of intentions this way, repeating step four, every single time feeling the further intention in the chain and asking yourself what's next. Do it until you can't answer the question from step four. It means that you have discovered the "original condition" or "core state": the ultimate, most important intention/goal you want to achieve.

For example, the whole process could look like this:

Problem: I'm totally stressed out before exams!

Question: What exactly do you want to achieve?

Answers: Prepare myself thoroughly. -> Intention 1: Pass the exams. -> Intention 2: Achieve the feeling of safety. -> Intention 3: Achieve the feeling of clearance. -> Original intention: Deep peace of mind.

The original intention is usually connected to a deep feeling of something, in a sense, a state of being: e.g. peace of mind, total calm, love, unity, presence, happiness. That's the state the part we are working with is following. It wants to achieve it by the action or behavior you want to change.

It's interesting as somehow this part of you concluded it will achieve that goal by acting or behaving like this, but in a large majority of cases the outcomes are totally opposite. By discovering that, you can change it.

The last step of this exercise is getting into that original intention fully and deeply. Now, thinking about each of these intentions from your chain of goals, starting from the end, think how having the Original Intention (and still feeling it at the same time) changes or enriches having each of these intentions.

So, for example, having the instance above for consideration, you should first access the state of deep peace of mind (by physical exercise, visualizations or meditation, preferably using all three of these ideas) and then think about how having this peace of mind modifies or enhances the feeling of clearance. Give yourself a moment to feel and imagine it, then proceed to the next intention (feeling of safety). At the end, think about how having the Original State/Intention will influence the behavior or action you are working on. Try to fully feel every single intention, while being entirely in the Original Intention, and imagine for a moment how it changes every ring/step in your chain of goals. At the very end, pay attention to how your approach to the behavior or action you are working with has changed. You are probably looking at it differently now.

Remember, resistance may appear during the process. Your subconscious mind may protest at some point, for example, saying, "But you can't be entirely happy!" Then, see this objection as a part of yourself and ask it what precisely it wants to achieve by this protesting and start this exercise over again, this time with this new part. Once when you're done with it, go back to the place where you've previously stopped.

I'd like to note that this isn't a typical intellectual or logical process. It's mainly about exploration and examination of your interior. When answering the questions in this technique, listen to your intuition, not your logical mind. It's very important as we are working with your subconscious and what's sitting deep inside of you, not with your rational thinking.

Some people, on the other hand, are not sure if they are going to get any answers using this method. Don't worry about it—when you're turned towards your interior, you will get your answers quickly. Sometimes they will come to you as a premonition, sometimes it will be an image or symbol, sometimes a memory, internal dialogue or a sound. Set yourself to listening and something will surely appear. Only then will you verbalize it and write it down on a sheet of paper.

Regular practice of this technique will enable you to go through it quickly and easily. You can also print the steps of this technique and use them only when you feel you need them.

How to Increase Your Self-Awareness

How well do you understand your character, emotions, motivations, strengths, and weaknesses? Self-awareness helps us understand what we are and what other people see in us. It also helps determine how similar or different we are from others.

Emotional intelligence promotes self-awareness. Some of the advantages of being self-aware include:

- Finding yourself

- Expressing yourself

- Understanding others

- Practicing empathy

- Having positive relationships

- Having clarity of mind

You get to develop your self-awareness through introspection. This is all about questioning your motivations – why you act or think in a certain way. Some of the questions you may ask yourself include:

- Why do you value certain things?

- Are you living responsibly?

- Are you moral or immoral?

- Why do you love certain things/people?

- Why do you hate certain things/people?

Here are some of the tips for increasing your self-awareness:

Try new things

When you seek new experiences, you're definitely going to learn a thing or two about yourself. Sometimes, it takes a change of environment, or a change of routines, to gain a new perspective on your strengths, weaknesses, emotions, and overall character. Exploring new things is a way of stretching your limits and stepping out of your comfort zone. One of the commonest methods of seeking new experiences is traveling. When you travel, you get to meet people from different cultures, and their way of life might force you to look at yourself in a new light. Traveling also has a calming effect on your mind and can promote clarity of thought.

Keep a journal

Get in the habit of writing down the various emotional states that you go through during the day, as well as their triggers. This will help you assess your emotional nature, and more importantly, it will put a timeline to your emotional states.

Meditate

A favorite exercise of yogis, meditation is truly a great practice for increasing your self-awareness. The premise behind meditation is that achieving a calm mental state multiplies your odds of reaching your goals. The classic yoga pose is made by sitting on a firm surface and placing each foot on the opposing thigh. Then you have to perform a breathing exercise that is aimed at eliminating the noise off of your mind. Meditation increases your ability to focus on your internal facets and thus helps you attain a clear understanding of the person that you are.

Know your strengths and weakness

Having a clear understanding of areas that you're weak and strong in is a great step towards increasing your self-awareness. This is important because after knowing your strengths, you can seek more ways to capitalize on it. On the other hand, knowing your weaknesses can encourage you to do something about it. For instance, if you have a weakness for binge eating, and it is showing in your waistline, it may affect your self-image. And so, through introspection, you might be able to identify the link between your binge eating and your self-esteem issues and perhaps cut out the binge eating and turn to healthy meals and workouts to get the body that you want. Finding out your weaknesses and strengths is a continuous process.

Know your emotional triggers

Emotions are merely the brain's way of trying to pass across an important message. There are certain things and events that cause the brain to activate the correlating emotion. It is critical to understand the various causes of your emotions. If you have gone through trauma, obviously you are emotionally scarred. Whenever you come across an event that is even loosely associated with the trauma, the bad emotions come rushing back. For instance, if you were once sexually assaulted on a dark road at night, you might find yourself getting anxious every time you're walking along isolated and lightless paths. Becoming aware that this anxiety is merely a warning that your brain is trying to send might help calm you down.

Reflect on your life

Get in the habit of taking stock of your life. This practice should be done on a daily basis. For instance, you may elect to reflect upon the day's events before you sleep. This will help you identify the areas where you have performed well, underperformed, or outright tanked. It will grant you the insight to sharpen your weak areas and capitalize on your strengths.

Avoid being narrow-minded

A narrow-minded person hardly sees the sense in what other people say, thus closing off any chance to expand their knowledge. However, if you want to increase your self-awareness, you must learn to open up your mind. There are various things you can learn about yourself if only you're open-minded. This is critical especially when it comes to accepting parts of yourself that you consider unbecoming. With an open mind, you also get to change your way of thinking and free yourself from frustrations.

Ask for feedback

As much as you may not want to admit it, sometimes people see things in you that you cannot see yourself. And so, you may want to hear what these people think about you, but take care that you ask people who have your best interests, people who want to see you make progress. When you solicit people's opinions, you make yourself vulnerable because their feedback might hurt you. But you should be open-minded enough to allow criticism, as this is the only way to grow. With the right feedback, you will realize the areas that you have to work on.

Set boundaries

You have to learn to set boundaries to develop your self-awareness. Setting boundaries is a way of respecting your time and showing people that you have goals to achieve. It regulates your behavior and guides you in the best manner possible. Setting boundaries and following through with the implementation takes courage and the support of other people. It is one of the critical things in understanding your limits.

Chapter 5: How To Get The Best Out of What You Have Learnt On EQ

In the 60s, renowned psychologist Walter Mischel did an experiment to observe how four-year-olds controlled their impulses. He put the children in a room and offered each a marshmallow. But there was a hook. He stated that he'd be going out to run an errand and that when he comes back, he will give another marshmallow to the children who don't eat their first marshmallow; however, it was still okay if they choose to not wait for him and eat their first marshmallow anyway.

After he stepped out, most of the kids started feasting on their marshmallow. But a small percentage of the children resisted the urge to eat their marshmallow and chose to wait for Mischel to come back and give them another. In the meantime, these kids performed various activities to avoid temptation, like walking around the room, covering their eyes, putting their heads down, and singing.

Many years later, when the children were in high school, remarkable differences were found between the two groups. The kids who had shown restraint over their impulses seemed more socially confident and well-adjusted compared to their low-willed counterparts. On the side of academics, the kids who held out scored an average of 210 points higher in their SAT.

What can be inferred in this experiment is that there's a huge correlation between delayed gratification and achieving success.

Motivation

In today's society, there's too much noise. Everywhere you turn, someone is trying to get your attention and distract you from what you're doing. Most people find it hard to stay "hungry" for their goals. They get carried away by other thrills. But a person who can manage their urges is in a position to keep fighting for their goals, as they know too well what they stand to gain. Since they have an understanding of this pleasant feeling and the sense of fulfillment that awaits them on the other side, it motivates them to carry on in their pursuit of success.

Good leadership

Success doesn't have to be one-dimensional. For a leader, the real measure of success is not when they reach their goals – it's when their followers reach their goals. As a leader, you have to be able to set good examples. This calls for great self-awareness and consideration on your part. When you set a good example, your followers can adapt to your ways and thus create an enabling environment for accomplishment. It takes a person who can delay gratification to lead by example.

Gratitude

It can be difficult to show gratitude if you're used to instant thrills and taking the easy way out. Actually, people who like having it easy tend to be entitled. On the other hand, people who can delay their gratification tend to show gratitude to both themselves and other people. This is because they achieve their goals by making plans and putting in the effort. For instance, such people tend to have a great appreciation for their money, and they ensure that they are careful about the things that they buy. They also appreciate people who commit resources to their projects, e.g., employees.

Sense of fulfillment

If you constantly make poor decisions, it doesn't necessarily mean that you're not aware of what you're doing. Most people are. For instance, if you decide against paying your child's school fee so that you can acquire your favorite item, you obviously know that you have done poorly. These bad habits tend to compound, and the resultant guilt can crush your soul. But a person who can control their impulse is careful about the decisions they make, financially or otherwise. In the end, it gives them a sense of fulfillment just knowing they took the best decision that there was.

Hard work

In this era of seeking instant thrills, it can be hard to get anyone to invest the time and resources required to achieve a desired outcome. Many people tend to seek the easy way out, and this usually leads to mediocrity. However, a person who can reign in their impulses is much more likely to invest the time and resources to achieve the desired outcome.

Learning to keep from gratifying your every want will instill in you a sense of discipline. For instance, when you challenge yourself into making the best of your income opportunities, you will have an appreciation for your money, and you might be able to see the advantage of saving over mindless spending.

Hard work teaches you how to prioritize and set goals. When you work within that framework, you tend to achieve more and become mindful of your habits. It takes a combination of various productive habits to eventually realize success.

Healthy lifestyle

If your health is failing, it can be difficult or outright impossible to achieve your goals. While deteriorating health is caused by factors both within and without our control, taking your health in your hands is a major step that asks for commitment on your part. For instance, if you have an alcohol problem, it can be difficult to give it up, and it will thus keep compromising your health. But if you have it in you to delay gratification, you will understand the long-term importance of giving up your alcohol habit. This mentality sets you up for success.

Improved finances

Most people lack financial discipline. That is why they spend their hard-earned money on things that they don't really need and end up burying themselves in debt. Poor financial decisions obviously affect the quality of an individual's life, and there's the possibility of what we call, "Financial ruin." However, a person who's mastered the art of delaying gratification will prioritize their needs. Their money only ever goes into what they really need, and such habits shield them from getting bogged down by debts or straying into financial graves. People who have a hold on their feelings are in a much better position to advance financially.

Guidelines on Managing and Expressing Your Emotions

Emotions are powerful biological forces that we cannot manipulate consciously. Once emotions get involved, things become complicated. Here are some important tips to adhere to to manage and express your emotions appropriately.

Master the art of timing

When you are pressed emotionally, being considerate is the last thing on your mind. You are simply dying to let the other person know what you're feeling. Emotions have a way of pushing all our wrong buttons, causing us to become impulsive in our decisions, and before we know it, it is over just as quickly as it began. Then we are stuck with the consequences. But, to communicate your emotions meaningfully, you have to ensure that the timing is right.

For instance, if your boss has done something that has triggered you, the last thing you should do is to storm into his office when he's in the middle of a meeting with other high-rank officials. You want to make sure that the environment in which you're communicating your emotions is an enabling one. This increases your odds of achieving the outcome you had planned.

Have a healthy outlet

In as much as you have to practice restraint where your emotions are concerned, it is also important to have an outlet lest you become an irritable person. When you bottle up emotions inside, you risk having it burst out one day, and woe unto the person on the receiving end. Obviously, this would defeat the purpose of practicing restraint considering that you have overreacted. One of the best outlets for your emotions is engaging in a physically-taxing activity like exercising and training.

Spend time in nature

Our environment has a big effect on our emotional states. If we live or work in chaotic places, our emotions are more or less going to take on that tone. Taking time to be surrounded by nature has a calming effect on your emotions. You could take walks in nature parks, hike, or hunt in the forest. This could help raise your spirits and release all the bad emotions.

Keep the big picture in mind

If you fail to get a handle on your emotions, you run the risk of throwing the baby out with the bathwater. Sometimes, you may get stuck in an unpleasant situation and feel like letting your emotions explode. Try to be wise enough to keep the bigger picture in mind. First ask yourself, what's your agenda? And how are your actions helping that agenda? For instance, say your teenage daughter is driving you up the wall. If you become hostile with her, she may end up cutting off ties with you, thus killing off any chance of you getting to guide her through life.

Learn to distract yourself

An emotionally intelligent person is aware of his emotional makeup; i.e., how their body responds to various stimuli. At the onset of an unpleasant emotion, rather than entertain it, learn to distract yourself. For instance, if you were working on a serious academic project and a very attractive person of the opposite sex stumbled by, you might get aroused and experience passionate feelings. Well, sexual emotion is not bad in and of itself, but considering that you're doing an important academic project, you might want to banish that sexual emotion.

You can achieve that by distracting yourself – engaging your mind in other activities. You may not have the ability to decide which emotion to experience, but when you pay less attention to a particular emotion, it tends to subside. However, if you lend your attention to a particular emotion, you tend to fuel it and end up increasing its potency.

Never react immediately

Whenever you experience a massive emotional trigger, be careful not to give an immediate response. This will give you time to assess the real situation and come up with the perfect plan. When you give an immediate emotional response, chances are the outcome will be less than desirable. For instance, if the actions or words of a person have triggered your anger, don't erupt in an outburst. This will get your aggressor worried about your next move. Meanwhile, you can be devising your comeback plan, or choose not to do anything at all. When you're consumed by an overpowering urge to give an emotionally-charged response, both your heartbeat and breathing rate will go up. Learning to control your breath can help in regaining your calm.

Communicate well

It doesn't matter what your intentions are, but if you cannot get around to communicating well, you'll have little chance of making progress. For instance, if you are agitated and have to face someone to resolve an issue, your verbal and nonverbal cues will play a critical role in how your message will be taken. Use a pleasant tone and ensure that you engage in active listening. Regardless of how powerful your emotions might be, there are always the right words to capture perfectly what you feel.

Practice honesty

Honesty is indeed the best policy. What's the purpose of expressing yourself in the first place if you're not going to be honest about how you feel? You should at all times ensure that you communicate your emotions in a manner that's as honest as possible, simply because that is the best way for you to get an honest reply. For instance, if someone at work did or said something that left you with a bad taste in your mouth, you might want to walk up to them and express how their actions or words made you feel. How they react is not in your power, but when you take the initiative, you will at least be on the right path to making things right again.

Practice mindfulness

Learn to stay aware of what is going on in your environment. This can only be achieved through mindfulness. When you get in the habit of being interested in other people, you create avenues for channeling positive emotions. We live in a world of pain, and so many people are in need of kindness. It is through mindfulness that we get to show our positive feelings to the world.

Chapter 6: The Past With Its Anchors

On EQ

Take a moment to reflect on your past. What do you see? Is it a source of strength and useful experiences for you or rather a source of recurrent pain and suffering?

We often hear confessions like, "These memories keep returning." "I regret what I did a few years ago." "How do I stop thinking about it?" Luckily, there's an effective way of dealing with your memories.

How old are you? Even if you're still young, you've surely been through a lot in your life already. Some moments were great, magnificent, worth remembering, whereas you would surely be eager to pay lots of money to have forgotten some of those less fortunate moments. Which of these memories take up most of the space in your mind?

There are people in this world who focus all their attention only on the unpleasant memories from their past. The more they want to forget about them, the bigger impact these thoughts have on them, and the more frequently they return. They experienced something unpleasant once and then they experience it again, again and again, ad infinitum, spending crazy amounts of time every day thinking about these past events and situations. They spend their entire lives thinking about the past.

It's exactly as if someone was driving a car looking in the rearview mirror all the time—not only is it impossible to reach the destination that way, but also, it's extremely likely to cause some serious accidents. The rearview mirror is very useful, indeed, but only to look at it occasionally to find what's necessary at the moment. Still, you have to look at what's in front of you all the time. That's the only way to drive your car safely to your destination.

Remember what you were doing yesterday at this hour? This recalled memory will probably come together with a certain image. When did this image appear? Here and now. So, does the past exist anywhere else other than outside of your head? NO. The past is nothing more than your imagination—a mind creation, collage of images, sounds and feelings. Just like a video recording. Is what you see on the recording real? Is it happening? No. It is only a reflection of reality. Not reality itself.

Let's state this again: the past does not exist. It is only a record in your head, in the form of multi-sensory memories. Why should you be worried so much about something that doesn't exist anymore? Why would you waste your life away focusing your attention on a videotape, on a stretch of reality which is recorded?

Think how many useless video recordings you keep in your head that do nothing but hold you back. Put them aside or you will go through all these negative emotions again and again, doing to yourself again what already ended a long time ago.

You can look at your past from many different perspectives. You can define it as a heavy burden you must bear until the end of your life or as very useful baggage of experiences, from which you will reap the wisdom just when you need it. Even the worst experiences can be viewed as a source of priceless teachings, which will provide you a helpful hand and direction sign on a desert in every difficult life situation.

When I sometimes work with people, I often come across those who regret what they have done in the past. I ask them, "Would you want to be in some other place in your life, different than you're in right now?" In most of the cases the answer is "No." Then I tell them that every single element of their past life contributed to the fact that they now are where they are. It's like in the movie The Butterfly Effect. Appreciate every single experience from your past, because even the unpleasant ones can prove as a useful source of skills and knowledge to you.

I recently talked to a businessman who told me a story of how once he lost huge amounts of money when his own co-worker robbed his office. He couldn't get over it for a long time and he couldn't let go of his anger and resentment. He really wanted his revenge, but finally, after some time, he decided to change his point of view to cease his suffering. He told me he now looks at this unfortunate situation as one of the most valuable lessons in his life. He's even grateful he got cheated, because now he pays more attention when picking new co-workers and cares much more about the safety of his business, thanks to which his new company grows much faster.

You can reframe every single memory like that. Everything is a matter of your perception. Looking from an entirely different perspective, you will feel totally different emotions. Always choose the perspective that is better for you. Change your view of certain situations and you will free yourself from excessive suffering.

Ask yourself these questions: Was what happened definitely a bad thing? Even if it was, what good can it bring into my life? What lesson have I learned? The answers will surely come and that's the moment when you start changing your detrimental perception of your past.

Mind you that liberating yourself from unpleasant memories doesn't mean erasing them from your life. They are, in a way, a part of who you are. You don't need to forget about where you came from and how you became the person who you are now. Your task is only to gain distance from what has happened, so that you can free yourself from the negative impact of these memories. It's about you learning how to look at the past situation without thinking, "Man, that was so horrible!" Instead, think, "What can I learn from that?" Once you get rid of the negative impact, it will be much easier for you to reap reward from the experiences you gathered during all those years.

Once you have come to an understanding of that, you will suddenly realize that all people's chances are equal. Their past doesn't really matter that much. It's not about where you came from, it's about where you're heading. Where you grew up, what kind of childhood you had, what parents you had and which school you attended doesn't have to affect your future at all.

It is extremely important for you to know your past doesn't have to equal your future.

The decisions about your future are always made here and now. Always make them taking your past experiences into consideration, but, before all, consider who you want to be in a month, one year, five years, etc.

There's one NLP exercise I'm going to show you that will help you to finally deal with all your negative memories. You will be able to start over again, leaving all your burdens behind and finally looking ahead with your chin up.

To begin, take a sheet of paper and start with writing down all the memories you can access in the form of keywords. Gather all the thoughts about your past that keep returning and inflicting bad emotions.

Then, pick one at a time and apply the NLP technique presented below. It is very important that you work on every single bad memory, once and for all, liberating yourself from all these returning thoughts about your past.

Perceptual Positions

Perceptual Positions in NLP refers to considering a situation from the first, second and third-person perspective.

The first position is your regular, daily experience about any event or experience. In the first-person perspective, or first perceptual position, you are completely connected with the experience through subjective filters. It is a personal, subjective experience that is free from another person's perspective.

The second-person perspective, or second perceptual position, is when you assume things from another person's point of view. Typically, salespeople, negotiators and counselors are remarkably good at the second perceptual position. They are processing information from the other person's perceptual experiences. This is done to empathize with the other person or understand their mind map.

The third-person perspective, or third perceptual position, is when you assume the role of an objective observer and consider perceptual experiences from an objective point of view or that of an external observer, much like watching a movie.

How do You Assume a Third Person Position?

Perform an activity, and during the activity move to a position that offers you a clear unobstructed view of the space where you just performed the activity. Take on a straight, upright position with shoulders pulled back.

Imagine watching yourself in the performance space. Doing it this way, you can give unbiased feedback. It is like watching a movie or theatre performance.

How Do You Assume a Second Position?

The second position is the position of modeling, learning and absorbing. It is like activating neurons in your nervous system that are dormant within the observer but boast of the same neuron functions as the neurons in the person you are modeling after.

The next time you find yourself in the company of a person you want to emulate, try these helpful tips:

•   Clear your mind completely.

•   Try to match your breathing rhythm or pattern with the person you want to emulate or empathize with.

•   Practice micro muscle mirroring. For example, if the other individual moves their legs, move your leg muscles slightly as if you are about to move your legs. Feel your leg muscles moving before lifting them. Practice this with full body movements.

The objective of the practice is to experience the world as if you are the other person. Imagine yourself assuming their body, so you become them.

Visualization

Since this book tells you to use visualization very often and because that's something some people have trouble with, I decided to add this chapter to help you better see your mental images. Again, it contains three practical and very effective exercises that will help you visualize better, with bigger intensity and the ability to take your visualization techniques to the next level. Visualization is a key to many tools, not only connected with NLP, but also with effective learning, goal setting, maintaining motivation and positive thinking, so it's worth it to establish this skill on a decent level!

Self-development can be defined as a pursuit of the desired condition. Since the state you want to achieve lies somewhere in the future, your ability to see what you want to achieve is one of the very crucial parts of the bigger picture.

Without a preview on how our lives should look like in the future, it's much more difficult to make real changes in the present. That's why rich and colorful visualizations that can totally devour you are so important. When you add sounds, smells, flavors and feelings, the references created in your brain can be so strong your subconscious will automatically focus all its attention on achieving your goal and will maintain that state for a long time.

Whether you have trouble with seeing the internal images at all or they get distorted and unclear, regular use of these exercises will enable you to create sharp, clear and detail-saturated visualizations.

Exercise I

·   Go to a silent place, ideally your room, with doors closed. Close your eyes and recall any situation from your life, preferably a nice memory. Don't try to see the images at this point, but focus on hearing sounds which accompanied that memory. Take a moment to listen to what happened there. What sounds are there? Is anybody saying anything? What's the manner, tempo and volume of their speech? Hear what you heard then.

·   Now, add a sense of touch to this. In your imagination, touch something that was there, any object, piece of clothing, whatever. Feel the surface of this object, its texture, temperature, weight. Get into that memory...

·   Now, add all the scents that were there. Feel the smell of the air... and then...

·   What do you see? See the images that appear. Maintain it and enjoy the view. You've just fully created your visualization.

This exercise is about activating any other senses than sight at first, which makes it much easier to bring back the image associated with that memory. It happens because every piece of information is saved in different parts of the brain. Not only does the information about memories contain visual data, but also auditory, sensory, etc., so that the increased activity in other parts of the brain helps you activate the sense of vision in your imagination and put it all together.

Exercise II

·   Choose any object from your room. It can be a phone, computer screen, book or anything else. Put that object somewhere close to you, so you can look at it freely. Observe it thoroughly for about five seconds.

·   After that, close your eyes and visualize exactly what you have just seen. Keep the image of this object as long as you can. If the image goes away, it doesn't matter. Open your eyes and start again.

·   After a few series, choose another object and repeat the same process—observe it for five seconds, then close your eyes and visualize it thoroughly.

·   Do this exercise five minutes a day, every day.

Practiced regularly, this exercise will give you the ability to create clear and accurate images on demand. It's just a matter of training—you will see that day after day the visualizations will be becoming increasingly natural for you.

Once you master bringing back the images of objects you normally see around you, modify it and create imaginary things in your mind.

Create abstractions of various kinds and keep them in your imagination as long as possible.

Exercise III

· Open a book, preferably a fiction story you like. Randomly pick a page and start reading.

· After a few lines, stop reading and close your eyes.

· Start imagining what you have just read about. Try to notice as many details as possible: people who are there, environment in which they are, the words they speak.

· Create this visualization for a minute, then go back to reading.

· After another few lines, close your eyes and start creating inner images again. Repeat this for about five minutes.

· Practice daily.

Literature is often rich in colorful, detailed descriptions that many times help improve imagination. The fact of reading about what's in the picture automatically creates the picture itself. In this exercise, you will additionally be able to consciously focus on that visualization, seeing many more details.

You can use the exercises above together or you could also pick one or two of them, the ones that suit you the most. Remember to practice regularly. It's like riding a bicycle — once you learn it, you will always be able to do it, as it will become perfectly natural to you. The ability to get into rich visualizations is a key that opens many self-development doors. You will finally be able to visualize a successful future, get rid of bad memories using NLP, remember difficult things using memorization techniques and do many other useful things.

Change of Personal History with NLP

1. Identify the memory you want to work on. If it's a situation you experienced more than once, pick the memory of the time when you experienced it for the first time. Close your eyes and imagine this situation as thoroughly as you can. Then, get into that memory as deeply as you can, feeling all these emotions that you then felt. Proceed to the next step once you're already immersed in that situation.

2. Now, break the state—do and think about something totally unrelated to that situation for a few minutes. Check your e-mail, cuddle your cat, count fruits in your kitchen or do anything else.

3. After five minutes, return to the technique and think what resource you'd need in that situation to make it a satisfactory experience instead of an unpleasant one—resource being an emotional state, skill or a certain belief. Maybe it could be the feeling of trust, being loved, self-confident or certainty that the other side had good intentions? Choose the resource that would entirely change your perception of that bad situation.

4. Focus on remembering if you had any situation in your life when you had this resource, fully and entirely? For example,

when you really felt loved or self-assured? Pick certain memories that will bring you the desired emotional state. Close your eyes and bring back exactly what you then saw, felt and heard. Get into that memory and recall all the emotions that were there. Once you can feel them fully, create the so-called "anchor" for the state—you need to establish a stimulus that will be connected to that feeling in your mind. I prefer kinesthetic anchors. You can, for example, touch the back of your hand with your fingers, grip your wrist a little bit or lightly pinch your ear. It should be unique, something you're not used to doing daily, such as scratching your nose.

5. Once you do this, break this state again. Then, close your eyes and go back to the negative memory, but this time see it as "dissociated", that is from the spectator's perspective (as a "third person"). Launch your anchor with the positive resource and watch yourself and the whole situation from aside. See how your entire behavior changes once you achieve the state you needed. See how the whole situation is changing along with the other people's behavior and your perception of that situation. Anchor that feeling.

6. Now go back to the beginning of that situation and watch it again, this time "associated"—from your own eyes' perspective. Launch the positive anchor again and see how the situation is going once you've obtained the necessary resources. What is different in your perception of this situation? How's your behavior and other people's behavior

changing? Give yourself the time to watch this situation until the end, then establish an anchor.

7. Check the effects. Bring back the feeling without launching the anchor and observe how the memory had changed. If you're still not satisfied with the change, go back to step 3 and go through the process again, this time choosing a different resource. If the negative emotions are gone—congrats!

Once you have worked through every single unpleasant memory, you're ready to take the next step. If you really want to bring back your memories, only go through the positive ones, the moments that give you joy and happiness.

The best solution is to move most of your thinking to the present and future. This kind of approach will give you more power and motivation and much more pleasure from living every day!

Dealing with Your Past

If you are still living in painful memories or carry any emotional baggage from the past, you are not paving the way for an emotionally healthy and balanced future. You'll have a hard time creating a happy and positive life ahead of you if you are still wrestling with the past. When you accept the past rather than obsessing about it, and deal with it, you are creating avenues for a more rewarding life.

Here are a few brilliant tips for dealing with the past and living a more positive, balanced and emotionally fulfilling life:

Acknowledge Past Challenges

Unresolved experiences of the past can create not only lasting physical damage but psychological consequences as well. Don't let these destructive emotions of shame, guilt, regret, revenge, etc. breed inside you for long. Learn to come to terms with these emotions so as to not let your present or future be affected by them.

Don't pretend that you are not affected by these events. You won't be in a position to get over it if you pretend that it didn't happen. Try to acknowledge and allow yourself to feel everything that you felt in the past (and still feel).

For instance, if you feel an overpowering emotion triggered by memories of the past, instead of curbing the feeling, step away for some time. Use this time to reflect on your emotions and how they impact you. Once you are done reflecting upon and feeling the emotions, get back to what you were doing. The consequence of past actions can be very powerful, especially if you are without a support system.

At times, the trauma from past actions is so overpowering that it impacts our relationships. Past trauma can also prevent you from fulfilling your goals. This affects not just your present perspective about life but also your ability to deal with challenges in life.

Understand that There's No Way to Change the Past

There is nothing you can do to change the past. As much as you wish to, you can't do anything to change events or people. The best way to manage a painful past is to tell yourself that it can't be changed now, accept it and change the way you perceive it.

There are many things that are outside our circle of control. However, the way we react to them is something that is still in our hands. We can either live in the past and ruin our present and future, or we can choose to learn from the past and move on. Even though plenty of circumstances are beyond our control, accepting these events as being a part of life is something that is completely within our realm of control.

The past cannot be revisited, but perception about it can be changed. If you don't stop obsessing over the past, the hurt will spill over and damage future experiences.

Direct your efforts towards accepting the past and offering forgiveness to the ones who have hurt you. You don't do this for them; you do it for your own peace and well-being. You give forgiveness to let go of the past and move on. Feel the emotions you want to feel and then let go after a point.

Try to remind yourself that hanging on to these destructive emotions will only end up harming you. Acknowledge the negative emotions and seek compassion for others as well as yourself. Gather all the strength to forgive everyone who harmed you.

Don't expect this to be an overnight process. It will differ from person to person and may take time.

Spend Time with Different People

Spending time in the same setting with the same people where you experienced negative past emotions will only trigger more of the same reactions. Instead, change your setting or spend time with a different group of people who are supportive, inspiring and positive. A powerful social support system can safeguard you from damaging experiences.

Support other people around you who are feeling low to derive strength from their situation and support them. Volunteering is one of the most wonderful ways to let go of a painful past and build a positive and constructive present which will serve as a foundation for a good future. It will also be a great way to interact with a new set of people. When you see other people's vulnerabilities, you become more thankful for your blessings and learn to cope with your troubles.

Seek the Help of a Professional

If you are feeling overwhelmed by your past and nothing else seems to work, seek the help of a professional counselor or therapist. There are instances when experiences can be devastating and can threaten to change your entire life ahead. In such cases, professional intervention is required. Talk to therapists who will help you with a series of therapies to move on from the past.

If nothing else, simply talking to a professional will help you see things from a more objective perspective.

Examine Your Social Circle

Consider moving away from friends who compel you to live in the past. Your immediate social environment will play an essential role when it comes to helping you let go of the past. It also defines who you are and affects your experiences. An encouraging, positive and supportive social circle that doesn't make you stay in the past can change the way you look at things.

I would recommend spending time with people who make you laugh or help you feel good about yourself. Stay away from folks who encourage negative habits or make you feel miserable about yourself. These are the type of people who will only stop your emotional growth or development. For instance, friends who constantly try to put you down or keep reminding you of the past may not be good news. Try making new friends in a different setting. This is will get you out of your comfort zone and facilitate personal growth.

Try new hobbies with new friends. Join a hobby group on social media or a local hobby club where you can interact with people who share similar interests. Fresh directions in life can open avenues you hadn't thought were possible earlier.

Systematic Desensitization

Systematic desensitization is a technique through which you are gradually relieving yourself of a potentially destructive situation with a series of relaxation techniques. The objective is to be at ease while exploring different stress relief methods.

Start with simple relaxation techniques such as deep breathing, exercising and meditation. Each time you find yourself exposed to a situation that stresses you as it reminds you of a past experience, you can practice these relaxation techniques to stay calm. The idea is to progress at your pace without rushing yourself to eliminate the pain. You should be able to engage confidently in situations that cause you distress over a period of time

For instance, if you had a terrible experience while addressing an audience on the stage earlier, you may avoid all opportunities to speak on stage. A past experience comes to haunt you each time you think of going on the stage. Get past this by actively opting to address an audience. Start with a small group of friends or co-workers in a meeting room or your home.

Employ relaxation techniques each time you find yourself being a bundle of nerves before speaking. Gradually, go with a bigger audience. There will come a time when you will be completely confident about addressing an audience without any fear. Keep going slowly, steadily and consistently. It may not be easy in the beginning, but eventually, you'll gather the confidence to master the art of speaking to an audience without being nervous.

The Art of Forgiving People

Forgiving people is important for emotional and spiritual growth. Your negative experience of how someone has hurt you is nothing but a negative energy you carry in your mind. These feelings of anger, revenge, hatred, rage and more gradually take away your power to focus on constructive and positive things by occupying space in your mind. When you release it, you should award or gift yourself more peace. Here are some tips for practicing forgiveness and letting your mind be occupied by more positive emotions:

Learn to Let Go like Water

Don't be forceful or try to one-up people in pointless ego battles. Rather be like water that just flows. Be soft, accommodating, tolerant and flexible of other opinions rather than forcing your views on others. Instead of focusing on telling and talking, concentrate on listening. When someone says something that is contrary to your argument, say something like, "I've never thought about it like this before, thank you for introducing me to a new point of view. I'll sure think about it."

Don't Actively Seek Occasions to be Offended

Don't keep looking for opportunities to be offended. Many people spend a huge amount of energy looking for occasions to be hurt. It can be a discourteous stranger, a person swearing around you, someone disagreeing with your views on social media or just about anything that ticks you off. Become a person who isn't offended by the tiniest of things or a series of circumstances.

Focus on Being Kind Instead of Being Right

When your mind is consumed by revenge, you are actually digging a grave for yourself, too. Resentment is destructive for you. The world isn't always hunky dory. People behave the way they do because that's just how they are. That's how they believe they are supposed to behave, and there's nothing much you can do about it unless it's a legally punishable offense. However, processing your reaction is something you can choose.

Get rid of the need to prove others wrong or to reinforce the idea that something bad has happened to you.

Think of a scenario where someone hurts you by saying something offensive. Rather than harboring feelings of resentment, you just disconnect or remove yourself from the situation and choose to react with kindness. You choose to send energies of joy and forgiveness rather than reacting in a negative manner. This is something you can do to maintain your internal balance and harmony. Focus on being compassionate more than being right.

Don't Sleep Angry

Before going to bed, don't spend valuable time reviewing anything negative that you don't want to be reinforced in your subconscious because as we discussed earlier, the subconscious is the most active when we are asleep. Focus on positive and constructive thoughts just before going to bed rather than harboring hatred. If you have had an argument or disagreement with someone, talk to them and clear the air before going to bed. Focus on ending it on a positive note even if you don't wish to associate with the person in future.

Be grateful and peaceful in aligning with your values and who you are as a person. Associate with people who possess the same beliefs and ideals as you. You are in control of how your mind is programmed just before going to sleep, which means you should only focus on positive thoughts.

Think About How No One is Perfect

Think about the person who has hurt you. He or she is a human with his or her own strengths and shortcomings. They are acting from their own limited beliefs and personality traits, for which you don't have to punish yourself. Their frame of reference may not be the same as yours.

While you were feeling hurt, the other person is trying to meet their own needs. What was the need of the other individual? Why do you think they behaved in a hurtful manner towards you? This will help you consider things from their perspective or be empathetic towards their situation despite being hurt.

At the end of the day, when we learn to handle our own emotions, our capacity to love and to also forgive will grow as well.

Chapter 7: Commonly Asked Questions

and Answers

The following are questions set to determine the emotional intelligence and social skills of an individual.

If you started a company, what would be your values?

This question is aimed at finding out your ideals. Company ideals are just as important as company goals. Come up with values that are all-inclusive and that reward excellence. Show that you understand the critical role that values play in the success of a company.

What inspires you?

This question is aimed at digging the sort of person you really are underneath your casual look. Your source of inspiration pretty much sums up what kind of person you are. It tells the world if you're a serious person or a joker. Thus, always select an individual or a cause that is closest to your objectives.

How would you create a more rewarding life?

This question is aimed at challenging your creativity. The underlying assumption is that life isn't great, but it has to be made so using only the materials at your disposal. You might want to take a close look at your suggestions to make sure that they are workable ideas. Write down the steps of moving from an unrewarding life to a rewarding one.

What angers you?

The question is about finding out the various things that push your buttons. Everyone has them. But be careful not to come across as an extremely sensitive person. You want to mention a couple of things that irritate other people as well and use some creativity to include other bad behaviors and attitudes.

What is your idea of fun?

Even the top managers of fortune 500 companies have a fun side to them. When answering the things that you consider fun, ensure that you don't sound cliché. Try to be a little bit more creative and mention activities that are not quite in the mainstream. It lends some mystery to your image.

What are your thoughts on asking for help?

This question seeks to understand your perception of team work and collaborative efforts. Try to come across as being in favor of collaboration. Many hands make the duty light. Many minds make the problem small. The input of other people is critical to the success of an activity.

What are your achievements?

This is not your chance to toot your horn like never before. Mention the cool things you have done with your life, but ask yourself if your achievements are truly important or whether you're the only person that considers them important. It could save you a great deal of embarrassment. Also, be careful not to come across as someone who thinks he's better than everybody else.

How do you react to frustrations?

Nobody is safe from feeling frustrated, but everyone has their own way of dealing with it. This question seeks to gauge your capacity to withstand frustrations. You should come across as someone who keeps your head in spite of challenges. Don't indicate any negative behavior you usually engage in every time you're frustrated.

What are your goals?

This question aims to find out your ambitions. Try not to sound like a person who lives in a fantasy world. Your goals should sound achievable, and your goals show what kind of person you are, so you have to be careful that they are appropriate.

What are your strengths?

It takes a great deal of self-awareness to realize your strengths. Your strengths will define your capabilities. Articulate how your strengths may help you achieve your goals. It is not enough to mention your strengths – mention as well how you apply them in your day-to-day existence.

What are your weaknesses?

People are scared of being vulnerable even when they don't have to be. Accepting your weaknesses doesn't mean that you're broken beyond repair. It actually means that you're a strong person. A self-aware person will know their weaknesses. But don't drop your list of weaknesses as if it were a badge of honor. At least acknowledge that you're trying to turn your weaknesses into strengths.

What are your religious beliefs?

This question is not purposely for labeling the person's religious affiliation but for understanding their outlook on human existence. A person who is religious will tend to believe that there's a divine creator behind all life, whereas an atheist will tend to align with theories that defy the existence of a creator. Religious beliefs are critical because they inform a person's way of expressing themselves.

Do you have friends?

It might seem like a weird question, but it is actually crucial. Living without friends is not the best kind of life. It may indicate an inability to connect with other people and create meaningful relationships, which is not a great place to be in. If you have no friends, at least admit that you're looking for them; otherwise, refrain from declaring that you have no friends and are not interested anyway.

What is your most defining moment in life?

Various people have different experiences that they consider to have had the most impact on their lives. You want to pick an experience that really altered the course of your life. Perhaps you had not been a "serious person" before, but this experience forced you to start taking life seriously. It helps if your defining moment has a happy ending.

What are your vices?

Each person has their own vices, but whether they have the guts to openly admit to them is another story. Admitting to having vices makes you appear more human. You may reserve the discretion of going into specifics, but it is enough to mention that you engage in practices that are not necessarily productive.

How do you celebrate your victories?

When you achieve your goals, there's obviously tremendous joy, but is there a method to your celebration? Some people jump into an airplane and travel away to a foreign country, and others just want to meet their real or perceived enemies and crow with delight. Whatever the case for you may be, always bear in mind that your method of celebration also says a lot about your character.

Conclusion

This is an extremely vast subject, but the way that I have tackled it in this book is intentional. Emotional Intelligence is something you need to measure for yourself and it is only by being aware of your emotions and reading them in different circumstances that you can really get a handle on why you respond in a set way to given circumstance. When you know that, you are less likely to allow emotions to take over and will exercise your emotional intelligence to be able to control negative feelings toward yourself and toward others.

Emotional intelligence helps you to be able to face different circumstances and be able to look beyond the obvious. You will also find that as you meditate on a daily basis, your intuition will truly become honed. There is a very good reason to want to do this as well. Over the course of your life, you have been programmed by everything that happened in your life. If you watch TV, you get programmed into believing that certain products add to your lifestyle. If you watch too much TV of a mindless nature, you tend to become mindless and this exercise once a day will help you to come back into the real world and find the reality of life is actually much simpler than you may imagine.

Being able to read people because of your emotional intelligence also helps them. You will be able to diffuse bad situations and not fall into the trap of letting the emotions take over when there is always some sense of logic behind why everything happens. By analyzing and keeping notes of your emotional responses, you learn to harness the power of emotional intelligence, so that the next time a situation of that nature presents itself, you are ready and able to cope with it.

People say that emotions are there to protect us, although I would say that they are much more than that. They can also destroy us if we let them. However, when you are the driver in your life, rather than allowing your emotions to be just that, you start to see how to use your emotions to help you rather than to work against you. You will understand people better and have a wider perspective on life. You will be able to help people more because your open minded approach means that you have more solutions than most people. You will also find that you get to recognize those emotions that are helping you to grow as a human being and those which can lead to your destruction.

In this day and age, it's even more important that you harness what emotional intelligence you have since more and more people these days are suffering from the effects of stress and it's becoming worse, rather than better. Your emotional intelligence is what brings you back into this moment in time and allows you to see things from a more neutral perspective. You tend to be forward thinking and also know how to respond to people's weaknesses which strengthen you are an individual. You will also be able to recognize the signs of your own emotions trying to take control and will be able to stem them until you have found suitable solutions to your problems. Everyone is born with emotional intelligence. It is only life that takes it away. The way that you were brought up and the circumstances that surround your life play a huge role in how you manage to handle your emotions. When you investigate and start to understand the triggers that make you weaker, you are able to stem emotional overload and become stronger.

I wish you well in your journey and would suggest you read the book several times and implement the suggestions made within its pages if you want to increase your emotional intelligence and start to enjoy your life to the fullest.

P.S

I would really appreciate it if you could just share with me what you have learnt from this book, just one thing of value that you have implemented to your everyday life.

Please pop over to amazon and share it over in the review so that others can also know how you have benefited from this!

Thank you so much!

35879805R00087

Printed in Poland
by Amazon Fulfillment
Poland Sp. z o.o., Wrocław